The Associate Pastor

The Associate Pastor

Second Chair, Not Second Best

Martin E. Hawkins
with Kelli Sallman

BROADMAN
&HOLMAN
PUBLISHERS

NASHVILLE, TENNESSEE

13-digit ISBN: 978-0-8054-4064-5
10-digit ISBN: 0-8054-4064-X

Published by Broadman & Holman Publishers,
Nashville, Tennessee

Dewey Decimal Classification: 254
Subject Headings: CLERGY \ CHURCH ADMINISTRATION \ CHURCH STAFF

Scripture taken from the New American Standard Bible®,
Copyright © 1960, 1962, 1963, 1968, 1971, 1972, 1973, 1975, 1977, 1995
by the Lockman Foundation. Used by permission.

1 2 3 4 5 6 7 8 9 10 09 08 07 06 05

Contents

Acknowledgments

$\mathcal{A}$s once stated, giants are only dwarfs standing on the shoulders of giants before them. For my life I find this to be true.

During my earliest development in the home, my father, Rev. A. T. Hawkins, performed the accountability structure for all his children to grow. He was responsible for leading me to Christ, baptizing me, and caring for my welfare as his youngest child.

Later the mantle shifted to my growth and development at First Baptist Church Jericho, where Rev. W. D. Willis continued my father's thrust by giving me the initial opportunity to grow and serve as youth pastor and later as his assistant. Then I moved to Texas to inaugurate my biblical training. Dr. John Reed picked up the mantle of my academic pursuits and pushed me to continue until completion. His encouragement was most appreciated and needed.

Inclusive in the background of all my growth in Dallas, Texas, is Dr. Anthony T. Evans. His model, his method, and his example, both academic and experientially, were always present for twenty-nine years. The laboratory of church ministry he afforded me is the backdrop by which this book is written.

Yet my most special friend, confidant, and lover, Shirley Hawkins, was and remains the backbone to all that I accomplish. Thanks, Shirley, for allowing me to become all God intended.

My thanks to all of you and the host of people who make me successful daily.

Introduction

Associate and assistant pastors often struggle with the idea that because they play the second (or third or fourth) position in their church, they are only second best to the senior pastor. Many did not aspire to an associate position; rather, they accepted the "lesser" role as training—as a path to the senior or solo pastorate. In our current culture, the assistant and associate pastor positions often lack respect. Unlike a senior pastor, the assistant pastor faces lifelong questions from himself and the congregation: "What exactly do you do?" "Don't you want more?" "What's the next step in your career?"

One associate minister, feeling the burden of these questions wrote, "Most people still think in terms of having one preacher who has a bunch of helpers. The other ministers may be important, but since they aren't 'the main man,' well-meaning parishioners continue to ask associates, 'When are you going to get your own church?'"[1]

Due to popular (but not biblical) leadership styles, congregational attitudes, and job ambiguity, associate attrition rates remain high, and our churches suffer instability as associates change from one field or church to another. But even more troubling, men[2] who desire to serve the Lord are losing their passion, their self-esteem, and their purpose after only a few years. We're losing workers for the harvest!

A handful of writers have given voice to the idea that the associate and assistant pastor play second fiddle to the senior pastor. I believe that is how most of the world views the assistant—a man skilled enough for the ministry but not gifted enough for first place or head leadership—in other words, second fiddle, second class, second best. Most of the writers go on to say that *despite being second fiddle,* the associate should understand himself as a vital and necessary part of the overall harmony of the church. I believe the writers have stepped in the right direction, but they haven't traveled far enough. Most are hoping that with encouragement and spiritual discipline, associate ministers can "come to terms with second-fiddle status."[3]

After more than forty years in the ministry, I say, yes, associate and assistant pastors are vital and necessary to the church, but they are *not* second fiddles at all. Assistants and associates will never find the fulfillment of purpose God intended for them if they continue to think of themselves as playing second violin to the pastor. They are not second fiddle; they are second chair.

From the beginning, God designed creation with an order, a hierarchy. But it's a hierarchy that does not lessen the value and contribution of each member. Adam's headship over Eve did not diminish her importance or her ability to do what God intended for her. In fact, God made her *more able* to perform the role of helpmate than her spouse. She was the best person for that job. Moses' leadership over Aaron did not lower God's respect for Aaron; God used Aaron to establish the priesthood.

Even God's essence speaks to a hierarchy of role, and not of value, ability, or priority. In the Trinity, the Father enjoys a head position; yet, no believer can deny the absolute necessity and worth of the second person's work. No believer would call the Son, our Savior Jesus Christ, second best, or second fiddle—and not quite good enough for his own church! After many years of ministry, I have concluded that the same idea applies to the assistant or associate pastor. He is not the second best man; he is the number one man in a second position. Second chair is positional, not personal.

I won't fool you. Who wouldn't desire the extra respect, the nice car, the better salary of the senior pastorate? I'd take it in a heartbeat. I would! . . . But then again, I wouldn't, not if it means being outside the center of God's will for my life. Let me put it to you this way: the associate pastorate position is not second rate; our current understanding of the position is second rate. Do we really understand the role of the second chair?

I didn't. I grew up in the little town of Jericho, New Jersey, where the only people our church employed with pay were the pastor, the church secretary, and the musicians. My only exposure to assistant pastors were pastors in transition who came to help Pastor Willis, either on their way to getting another church or coming back from a church and before moving on to a pastorate. Therefore, I understood an assistant pastor to be a person who assisted the main pastor's needs for a time—not a full-time paid position, not a position to which God had called someone—a person who wanted to spend some time with the pastor, to visit the hospitals with him, and help him with funerals.

So while I was younger and at that church, that's exactly what I did. I assisted Pastor Willis. I grabbed his briefcase. I drove him here and there. At funerals, he led and spoke while I attended to the behind-the-scenes work. I never missed his preaching, and from time to time, he asked me to preach. That was my understanding of an assistant or associate pastor.

Then when I felt like God was seriously calling me to the ministry, I thought I would get some good training and become a pastor like Pastor Willis. I had no desire to be an assistant pastor. It didn't even occur to me to consider it as a full-time position. I moved to Texas and attended Dallas Theological Seminary. While there, I interned as an assistant pastor under Dr. Anthony Evans at Oak Cliff Bible Fellowship. His church was just starting out, barely budding from its ten charter members. I didn't know that

I would want to work with Dr. Evans long term, but after I went to all the churches in the area, I told myself that I'd rather start there with a new work and see what it was going to be. Then if I decided to change later, I would change.

Well, I never changed, and the rest is history. I was Dr. Evans's assistant pastor at Oak Cliff Bible Fellowship in Dallas, Texas, for twenty-nine years. Did I settle? Was I unable to achieve what I set out to be? Did I fail?

On the contrary! With the Lord's guidance, I stumbled into a fantastically fulfilling role that fit my passion and my design. And over the years, I discovered this new, evolving ministerial position—a position that in many ways takes a backseat to the senior pastor, but that is just as God honoring and worthy of a lifetime of service as is being the headman. Perhaps God has designed you for this role as well. For those of you elbow deep in ministry or just licking your lips to begin, do you know how God has designed you? Do you understand His calling on your life?

I wrote this book to share with you the insights I learned during more than a quarter century of being an assistant. It is my goal to bring respect and respectability to those called by God to be second, third, fourth, or fifth chair as associate pastors. I pray that by the time you reach the last page of the book, you will not only have gained an appreciation for the associate pastor role, but that you will also have reached a better understanding of how God is calling you.

Chapter One

Second Chair:
The Assistant Pastor's Role

*And He gave some as apostles, and some as prophets, and
some as evangelists, and some as pastors and teachers, for
the equipping of the saints for the work of service, to the
building up of the body of Christ; until we all attain to
the unity of the faith, and of the knowledge of the Son of
God, to a mature man, to the measure of the stature which
belongs to the fullness of Christ. (Eph. 4:11–13)*

String instruments are the heart of an orchestra. The violin section in particular is large and is split into a first violin section and a second violin section. The second violins add harmony to the string section while the first violins enjoy a more prestigious role. They not only play the melody, but they lead the way and establish the melody for the entire group. And the principal first violinist, the first-chair first violin, has an even more important role—managing and directing all the sections of the orchestra. He is called the concertmaster (or mistress).

The violins are considered a virtuoso instrument, and therefore the concertmaster gets to showcase his talent perhaps more than any other member of the orchestra. The concertmaster also gives the bowing before rehearsals and concerts—giving everyone the precise note to which they must tune themselves.

If you have ever attended a symphony, you'll know what I am talking about. Before the concert begins, musicians arrive on the platform and begin to warm up their instruments. It's a mess. Every musician plays just what he wants, and all the sounds crash into one another. But just before the conductor takes the stage, the concertmaster arrives, and the instruments quiet down. The concertmaster draws his bow across his violin, and the orchestra begins to play that same note. For a few moments, instruments here and there make adjustments until their note tunes perfectly with the concertmaster's. If the concertmaster has not tuned his violin precisely to the correct note, "concert A," the entire orchestra will amplify his flaw. He shoulders great responsibility.

When he feels that the orchestra has tuned itself well, the concertmaster quiets everyone in anticipation of the conductor. The conductor arrives, bows, lifts his baton . . . and expects as he brings it down that a beautiful sound will rise from the prepared instruments. This is the role of the senior pastor. He is responsible to the Conductor for preparing his congregation and bringing them into tune with the Almighty. He sets the tone for his church.

One reason the associate or assistant pastor role has been likened to playing second fiddle is because the senior pastor's role fits so well as the head "first fiddle" in an orchestra. The analogy works for the senior pastor position. But consider how the rest of the violin picture works: for the orchestra, anything less than concertmaster, whether in the second violin section or the first, is less than the best.

When an orchestra hires new violin players, the musicians must compete for the "chairs" they will sit in. Usually they will start near the bottom and have to work their way up. The chair each player sits in—first, second, third, and so on—*equals* his or her rank. The player receives his or her placement after being compared to everyone else. It's a placement that says, "All other things being equal, this musician has more skill and artistry than the musicians sitting in lower-ranked chairs but less than the ones above him." And because of the two violin sections, even *first* chair in the second section is considered second class (despite the fact that relatively few musicians in the world reach this distinction).

Therefore, everyone's desire, especially those just below the concertmaster in the first section, is to eventually "overthrow" the concertmaster and take that spot himself. Everyone wants to play the solos, to gain the spotlight, and become a household name.

This, too, may be the outlook of some people in the associate ministry: "When am I going to get his job? When am I going to get my own church, my own name on the marquis?" But it shouldn't and it can't continue to be our perspective of the assistant pastor's position. The analogy breaks down for associate and assistant pastors. It's not biblical. It's not healthy for ministry. The assistant pastor is not second fiddle. He's a highly skilled, highly needed member of a ministry team that labors to build Christ's church. But if we're not talking about second fiddle, what is second chair?

Second Chair: The Brass Horn

Consider the analogy of the brass horn. Unlike the string sections, the brass instruments do not duplicate one another's sound, but each chair within the section has its own part. Because the brass instruments have more volume, fewer are needed to balance the orchestra sound. Therefore, most orchestras use only two trumpets and two to four French horns. If the player's part is in the music, *he is necessary.* Unlike the competitive concertmaster's position, the first chair horn does not automatically receive his position because he is a more brilliant player than the second chair; instead, the first chair horn becomes first chair because he excels at the higher notes. He is gifted for that chair.

The melody is usually composed of the top half of the scale (such as a soprano often sings in a choir). So by default, the first chair plays more melodies and more solos *even though the second chair might be a steadier, more exquisite player.* The second chair excels at the lower harmony, and the lower harmony cannot be heard in its fullness without the leadership of the melody. Second chair, by necessity, is a team player, but he's a team player who is highly skilled and highly needed to support and fill out the sound of the melody. The second chair horn is second chair, *not* second best.

Second Chair: The Son

Humanly speaking, we naturally consider a boss, one above us in authority or someone who gets all the attention, as necessarily "better" in some way. This natural ranking overflows onto our perspective of the assistant. Can we avoid thinking in this manner when it comes to the ministry team? How can we in the ministry change our perspective about the associate's worth? Do we do away with the chain of command, since the hierarchy itself seems to cause much of the problem? I don't think so. I think we look at the best model of ministry and relationship that exists.

Perhaps the best analogy for how the multistaff should function relationally is the Trinity. The Father gives the order and vision, the Son obeys and serves, and the third chair, the Spirit, humbly makes sure that the work of the other two gets completed. They have a chain of command. In the midst of this chain of command, however, each member gives to the others the work best suited to that person, supplies the others with whatever they need, and honors the others over himself.

The Father accomplishes his work, his creation, through the Word and the Spirit. The Son glorifies the Father and acknowledges his headship, yet also receives and performs the headship of the church, which the Father has given him to manage. As unimaginable and beyond understanding as the Trinity is, its perfection lies in the honor that each member bestows on the others, that gracious insistence that each *is necessary.* God is not God without the second and third chair. I do not put anything past his ability, but how could he accomplish the cross without the Son to perform it, and the Spirit to guard all those who kneel before it?

When the church grows to need more than a solo pastor, the associate and the assistant—with all their special gifts and talents—*are necessary.* Can we learn to honor that position with the respect it deserves—as a vital, God-honoring, God-called leadership position in ministry?

God gave some as apostles, some as prophets, some as pastors and teachers—and dare I say he gave some as senior pastors and some as assistants—for the building up of the church to maturity in Christ. If that is true, if God gifted all these people and placed them in just the right role, how did we get to this place where we view associates as less than the best?

The Assistant Pastor's Beginnings

The church has always had assistant or associate pastors in some form or another but never so much as today. In the last half century, our idea of large has shifted. But as the associate pastor role has transitioned from volunteer or part-time to full-time to even full-time and managing his own staff, our concept of who he is and what he does has remained behind. Previously, most rural churches and other small churches had maybe fifty members. Churches with three hundred to five hundred members were considered large and needed additional pastoral staff. This additional staff might have been called an assistant pastor, but also might have been "the part-time semi-retired minister of visitation, the youth minister, program director, the minister of music or a member who [was] an ordained minister but currently in a non-pastoral position."[1]

Today, while we still have small churches, and while churches above three hundred members will continue to need assistant and associate pastors, now we have the megachurch. The megachurch on the low side has one thousand members. On the high side, it might have twenty to twenty-five thousand, and the pastor who thought that he could manage the church body with part-time staff doesn't exist anymore. The pastor who is ministering to twelve or thirteen hundred people with only part-time staff might do well with what he can do, but he can't keep up with all that needs to be done. Burnout happens at a high level.

So now you have a senior pastor and assistant and associate pastors, some of whom fulfill roles traditionally separate from the main pastor like the youth minister or the minister of music. Yet other assistants and associates function as secondary ministers. They support and assist the senior pastor in his role, which has expanded beyond the capabilities of one person. It is concerning this new type of pastor that Donald Esa writes, "In many churches, the Assistant Pastor's position is an ambiguous role. Considerable attention has been given to the role of the senior pastor in a church. . . . However, very little has been written or taught in seminaries about the role of the secondary minister in a church. Hidden from the limelight, many Associate Pastors struggle in their positions to find fulfillment and significance in their roles."[2]

The lack of attention given by institutions and authors to the role of an assistant pastor gives the impression that assistant pastor positions are secondary in *importance* and preparation for them is not worthy of in-depth discussion typically given to other positions. Yet this conclusion is as far from the truth as my saying that the Lord God Almighty is not a God of grace! On the contrary, assistant and associate pastors have a great effect on the success of local congregations. Without them, growth becomes stunted.

Lord willing, the increase in church growth will continue. In the African-American community alone, there appears to be an outpouring of people of all walks of life who are seeking the Lord. Oak Cliff Bible Fellowship has experienced a phenomenal growth; it started in 1976 with ten people and now at the turn of the new millennium, it has about seven thousand people attending. Within a five-mile radius of Oak Cliff Bible Fellowship, at least ten other churches have a congregational size of one thousand or more members. This unusual growth pattern appears to have no end. At least five of these churches are building auditoriums large enough to seat three thousand or more.

In trying to provide an explanation for the exponential church growth experienced at Oak Cliff Bible Fellowship and other large African-American churches around the country, Dr. Evans postulated this response: "The African-American church has returned to the church that existed during slavery. During this struggle the church developed a holistic approach to its people and continued to be the institution of stability for a people who were disenfranchised. Today although the same institution of slavery has been removed, the area of technology can feel the push of an impersonal society. Churches in the African-American community have not lost the need for the central, dominant senior pastor and leader, but now are also being ministered to by multistaff, multifaceted programs."[3]

While slavery, of course, did not affect everyone in this country in the same way, the impersonal push of technology reaches everyone. People in general are gravitating toward churches that will allow them the freedom to minister, to use their gifts, and to connect with others. Although the sizes of the churches are growing, ostensibly making the experience more impersonal, the multigift, multistaff approach is doing just the opposite.

Brad Smith of Leadership Network, now residing in Dallas, Texas, summarized the four major movement influences of the church:

> The church growth movement emphasized cultural relevance, church planting, marketing techniques, user-friendly faculties and assimilation of visitors. The seeker sensitive movement has focused on cultural relevance, specially designed events that appeal to the unchurched, evangelism, and discipleship training for new believers. The contemporary worship movement has brought involvement of the laity in praise music and integration of teaching with worship. The small group movement has developed lay-led small groups for the pastoring and discipling of parishioners, and expansion of worship through decentralized leadership.[4]

Through these movements, the growing church is accomplishing God's command to make disciples. But at the same time, the growth of individual churches and specialized ministries is shifting solo pastors into the leadership of multistaff churches while creating a widespread need for second chair assistants.

The Assistant Pastor's Role

At this point, let me say that from here on out I will use the terms *assistant* and *associate* interchangeably. Although many churches give the terms separate and definite meanings, those meanings vary extensively from church to church, making it virtually impossible to give a definitive meaning that fits universally. For instance, at Oak Cliff Bible Fellowship I was the sole assistant pastor although we also have numerous associate pastors. My role fit directly underneath Dr. Evans, and I was responsible in his absence. Our associate pastors, on the other hand, are each more specialized in the areas they lead. But whether a church has associate pastors or assistant pastors, or a little of both, the assistant or associate pastor's position is a supportive leadership position.

The individual in this position has the primary responsibility to assist the senior pastor in creation, implementation, and management of specific functions designed to bring about the unity and maturity of the body of Christ. This involves working closely with the church's ruling board as well as the congregation. This position's duties can entail general responsibilities delegated by the senior pastor, the ruling board, or both. In other instances, the assistant pastor takes responsibility for specific areas of ministry such as education, outreach, youth, or worship. Although associate and assistant positions may vary by denomination, culture, and geographical location, they are, largely, the same position only redefined because of one or a combination of various responsibilities unique to an individual church.

The Assistant Pastor's Instrument

Because the assistant pastor's role varies, not everyone will fit into or arrive at the role in the same manner. Ideally, each man entering the ministry will understand his call, his passion, and his strengths. If you are currently in or preparing for ministry, I desire that for you. I want you to know your purpose in ministry so that you can fulfill God's call on your life in a way that brings him the most glory and honor. I want you to know that if God has called you to assist a senior pastor on your way to being the best senior pastor you can be, your apprenticeship is just as God honoring as your future leadership. And if God has called you to be a lifetime assistant, I want you to know that the call to second chair is just as God honoring as the senior pastorate. For you, it is not to be a stepping-stone to something better. It *is* the something better. It is your life's work.

As I have lived and studied the assistant pastor role for more than the last quarter century, I have seen a number of reasons for why a man takes an assistant pastor position. For clarity's sake, let's break down the assistant pastor role into three categories: the intentional assistant, the unintentional assistant, and the unintentional pastor.

Intentional Assistant

"You are to speak to him and put the
words in his mouth; and I, even I, will be
with your mouth and his mouth, and I will
teach you what you are to do." (Exod. 4:15)

The intentional assistant knows that he wants to be on
a staff. He's a leader—he has to have a desire to lead—but
he's not the senior pastor type. He knows he can lead people
under someone else's vision, but God has not gifted him
with the desire or passion to establish the main vision and
direction of a church. This person belongs in a supportive
leadership role. If you force him to take the main leadership
role long-term, he will flounder and lose his passion for
ministry. He will burn out.

Some intentional assistants do not prefer the pressure or
the spotlight of the lead chair. They don't want the solos.
Others don't mind the limelight—in fact, they probably
would thrive with the recognition—but their gifts and
skills fit the second chair best. An associate over a specific
ministry has the freedom to concentrate on his specialty,
something the senior pastor often doesn't have time for. He
can make sure that every visitor receives a warm welcome.
He can experiment with many different ways to reach the
community beyond the church. He can hone his artistry to
make the worship experience sweet nectar before the Lord.

Other times, the more general assistant knows that he
excels at providing a supportive base. He keeps the senior

pastor's melody afloat. He fills out the programs. He coordinates the staff and membership and helps align them with the senior pastor's vision. He follows through with all the care and administrative needs that the senior pastor can't get to and still finish his sermon preparation adequately. The intentional assistant is necessary for the senior pastor to function properly. No one will listen to the sermon if they are concerned that their children aren't satisfactorily cared for in the children's ministry.

Twenty years ago, a young man interned with Oak Cliff Bible Fellowship while he attended seminary. When he graduated, he left our church to follow another young pastor starting his senior pastorate in another area. Twenty years later, he's still there. And when I talk with him today, he still has the same passion that he did on the day he got out of seminary. "I don't want to pastor," he told me. "I want to work here in this church and assist the pastor." He understood his calling and design. He followed his passion. He has spent twenty years perfecting a role that he respected enough to commit to as his life's work. And he plays a great second horn.

Unintentional Assistant

> "Thus the LORD used to speak to Moses
> face to face, just as a man speaks to his
> friend. When Moses returned to the camp,
> his servant Joshua, the son of Nun, a young

man, would not depart from the tent."
(Exod. 33:11)

The *un*intentional assistant, however, fresh out of seminary takes on an associate position to transition himself before he takes a church. He looks on this role as an internship, whether it is a called one or not. Although he must function in the role of an assistant, he knows that this path will be short-lived. He wants a senior pastorate role. He has the passion, the calling, and the skills to be a good pastor. Trying to keep this man on staff after his internship ends will usually only disservice him and the staff he serves, because he will continually butt his head against the restrictions placed on his calling, his passion, and even his personality.

The church has room for this type of assistant, but he must take care not to disrespect the role he has selected while training for another. He must be open and honest about his true intentions, not only to avoid causing dissension, but also to gain the best training he can for his future responsibilities. This man *hires on* to play second fiddle. He needs to come in saying, "Let me lighten your load in these areas while you teach me to become a concertmaster." For a short time, this leader-in-training fills a dual role: (1) he learns to fulfill and appreciate the harmony of the second chair, and (2) he studies and practices first violin melodies.

I had a certain intern at Oak Cliff whom I knew would succeed in the pastorate. Why? Because everything I asked him to do, he did, and he did it with detail and on time. He showed humility and an ability to serve.

He walked around with me. He shadowed me when I went to the hospitals. He shadowed me when I officiated at weddings. He asked me all the questions—the good questions such as, "Why did you do it this way? Why did you change and do it this way? I thought it would be better . . ." And we talked about it. We rode in the car together and talked about ministry. On the way to the hospital, we talked about what Scripture we were going to use when we visited with the sick person. Perhaps a person had a particular kind of sickness, and I questioned the intern about what Scripture was appropriate for this situation. This intern was interested in learning by doing.

Every day I told him to sit in on board meetings to see how boards operate. I told him, "Boards are where you're going to make it or break it." He attended our elder board meeting, and he did everything he could do to make himself a good pastor while he was an intern. We knew he was going to leave, but he worked hard as if he were going to stay. And he made a contribution to our church. He set up a system for financial planning and a system for community work. Even though he was a student, even though he knew he would leave one day, he came to the church and went to work. And when it was time, God called him to a pastorate in Waukegan, Illinois. God ordained him to be a great pastor. He learned well *as an assistant*.

Here's an equally good but different example. Another

intern assisted me in the area of care and comfort. He targeted a specific area that he wanted to learn, and he rolled up his sleeves to gain wisdom under my mentorship. When it was time for him to leave our church, he didn't go into the regular pastorate; instead, he went to the army. He followed his calling to become an army chaplain, a leadership position analogous to the senior pastorate, but different—much more focused on care and comfort. And he told me that the work was easy because of what he had done while interning at Oak Cliff.

Occasionally, an unintentional assistant will not immediately recognize his own calling to the senior pastorate. Either through God's delay in making the call known, unfinished preparations, or a reticence to assume the responsibility, an assistant may find himself fulfilled in his role with no aspirations for the lead position. As we will see in future chapters, however, a mentoring pastor aware of the more common skills, personality types, and spiritual leadership abilities associated with both the senior pastor and the assistant pastor (allowing always for the Lord's creativity) should be able to identify those assistants who have a better affinity for the senior pastorate than the assistant role.

Of course, the senior pastor should not push these assistants out of the nest. He should take special care to prepare them well for flying in the lead. Then, when the Lord determines to reveal to these fledgling pastors their calling, they can transition to the front of the formation with confidence.

Men in this category or those who are not sure of their intentions should take note: it is vitally important under whom you intern. Not every assistant pastor has the opportunity or ability to teach a leader-in-training about the entire church like I did. Sometimes, interning under an associate will teach you a lot about music, worship, or children but not about the total church. If you think God is calling you to the senior pastorate, make sure you take on an internship that will expose you to the senior pastor's duties as well as the specific duties you will need to fulfill as associate. Even at Oak Cliff, I trained our interns conjunctively with Dr. Evans so they were fully prepared for their calling. Be honest about what kind of training you seek. Just don't expect to be senior pastor while you're an intern. Learn the role of the assistant, too—and learn to appreciate it.

Unintentional Pastor

"But there were some of them, men of Cyprus and Cyrene, who came to Antioch and began speaking to the Greeks also, preaching the Lord Jesus. And the hand of the Lord was with them, and a large number who believed turned to the Lord. And the news about them reached the ears of the church at Jerusalem, and they sent Barnabas off to Antioch." (Acts 11:20–22)

The third category is the unintentional pastor. This man becomes a senior pastor, but after two or three—or even ten—years, he is fired, he quits, or he realizes that he is not senior pastor material. I've seen this happen, and it can crush a man's spirit and his desire for ministry. He wanders around feeling not good enough—not good enough for the pastorate, not good enough for the church, not good enough for God.

Sometimes an assistant type must take the pastorate role at least temporarily to fill a void, knowing that this is not to be his life's calling. Other times, he has misunderstood his calling or his leadership skills, or perhaps he yielded to a congregation's pressure, listening more to them than to his own knowledge of his calling. While he was loved as an intern or supporting pastor, he finds he is not loved as the leading pastor. And sometimes, the unintentional pastor has followed the senior pastor track despite his skills because he was drawn to the power, the prestige, and even the paycheck of the lead pastor.

I have a good friend from South Jersey whom I felt all along should have been an assistant or on a church staff, but he pastored for seven years. It didn't really work out for him. It didn't seem to *ever* really work for him. He has great skills; he's a wonderful, godly man, but every day of his senior pastorate he struggled. He lacked passion. His congregation complained that he wasn't a good pastor. Why? God didn't design him to make daily the hard decisions of a senior pastor. God designed him as a tremendous support staff person.

When my friend talked to me, I told him, "You should have been on staff all along and been working on a team." So he did. For the last ten years he's been working as an associate. Now the people love him and the pastor of the church loves him because this was his calling from the beginning. Now he is at his peak effectiveness. He can glorify God with joy and passion.

Are you playing the right instrument? Did you pick up the violin because you thought "concertmaster = ministry" and never looked back? If you struggle daily to keep your joy—or your job—consider that you might fit better as a second chair brass or maybe even a small church percussion leader (the percussion player usually has to play all the percussion instruments—a jack-of-all-trades). Remember, the concertmaster would not have an orchestra without all these other vital players.

Other Categories

Of course, you can also make a case for other associate categories. Currently we're seeing the rise of what might be called the executive pastor. This pastor is in charge of the business of running the church, overseeing all internal administration. He takes care of the paperwork and the business management of the church. For some trained pastors, these administrative skills are far more developed than their spiritual leadership skills. Rarely, a trained pastor may be able to take this position with added spiritual responsibilities and do both well. Often, though, a theologically untrained businessman with a passion and affinity for the church fills this new and evolving role. Because this position usually lacks spiritual responsibility, it will not be a part of our discussion in this book.

Another category that I must note might be called assistant to the pastor. This position, in which I served fruitfully during my youth, usually does not involve a trained minister. Rather, it is a person who wants to spend time with the pastor and do things for him, whether it's to visit someone at the hospital, fetch a cup of coffee, or take the pastor to the airport. Much can be observed of the pastor's leadership and spiritual living through this role, and it is a useful position both for the young person considering entering the ministry and the pastor who has a busy schedule.

The assistant pastor at a small church also often finds that his role floats somewhere between the assistant pastor role and the assistant to the pastor responsibility. Sometimes, too, the assistant pastor at a larger church must bend to include some of these less-than-leadership tasks into his schedule. But by and large, the assistant pastor position and the assistant to the pastor are two entirely different functions. One is a professional position, and the other is a more functional role.

The Conductor's Prerogative

What each of these categories has in common—although the gifts and skills of the men differ greatly—is that each assistant pastor, no matter his future responsibilities, must learn to serve, to obey, and to trust the leadership under which God has placed him. Even the concertmaster must take his cue from the conductor. The Almighty gets the first and final say on our design and our position in the orchestra. But while the church currently looks down on the second chair, God values both the first and second chairs with the same priority.

Chapter Two

The Conductor's Viewpoint: The Priority of the Assistant

(ACCORDING TO GOD)

And a voice came out of the cloud, saying, "This is My Son, My Chosen One; listen to Him!" (Luke 9:35)

*Y*ou might have just read the title to this chapter and are muttering to yourself, "Hawkins, who are you to think you know the mind of God?" Well, I certainly wouldn't say that I do. After all, I've spent a lifetime just trying to know the mind of my senior pastor, Dr. Evans! But because we can know God's heart through his Word, we can see his intentional care and priority for the assistant.

Although the Bible does not explicitly define assistant roles as they exist today, both the Old Testament and the New Testament provide information about those who assisted the primary leader and God's purposeful calling on their lives. For comparison, let's first look at the care the Lord took in preparing one of the most important primary leaders in the Old Testament—Moses.

The Senior Pastor

Moses had an intimate relationship with the Lord while leading the people of Israel out of Egypt. He became a "senior pastor," so to speak, of dynamic proportion and influence. Deuteronomy 34:10 states, "Since then no prophet has risen in Israel like Moses, who the LORD knew face to face." So how did God prepare him?

God himself directed Moses' training for leadership. He used Pharaoh's murderous declaration against Hebrew baby boys to place Moses in the Pharaoh's palace. Moses received training, knowledge, and leadership skills from the Egyptians while at the same time he learned about his God and heritage from his nursemaid—his own mother.

After Moses fled from Pharaoh's wrath, God protected him in the wilderness and led him to his father-in-law Jethro for more training. In those years, Moses observed Jethro, the priest of Midian, ministering to his large family and the Midianites in a harsh environment.

Chosen Vessel

The Lord spent Moses' lifetime preparing him for his future mission. Then on the Horeb mountaintop, he called

Moses to his specific ministry. Did Moses get to choose which role he would play in God's plan? Did he choose the celebrity or his status in history? No. Actually, in spite of all of God's preparation, as Moses looked ahead to the tasks and the responsibility that the Lord placed before him, he balked. "Who, me?" he said. "Please, Lord, send whomever you wish"—and in a small voice—"but not me. I'm lacking in some things that might hinder your plan." If the Lord had let him, Moses might have turned God down! But the Lord didn't say, "Here Moses, you choose who you want to be and what you want to do. I'll just follow along." No! He said, "Moses, this is the work that I have prepared you for and uniquely suited you to do. Trust me and obey."

Power and Authority to Produce a Mission

The Lord God prepared, called, and supported Moses in the leadership role. God gave him the power and authority to ascend on Egypt with a special mission of emancipating Israel from the hands of the Egyptians. In the same way, God's call for every senior pastor includes the power and authority to perform his mission within God's plan. Moses had experienced the burning bush. His staff had changed into a serpent. He had received constant affirmation from God assuring victory. Yet Moses still shied away from God's plan for him. The senior pastor's call—the call to leadership, to shepherding, and to transmitting a vision for the church—can be very intimidating. After all, people's souls are at stake. He is to teach the incredible Word of God. And the senior pastor just might have to confront Pharaoh. Who in his right mind—who, having experienced discipline or learned humility from the Lord—thinks he has all the skills and the tools needed to do this job?

God cares who leads his people, and he knows we don't have everything it takes to do the job. It was his initiative and his choice to place Moses in that role in spite of Moses' weaknesses. He would provide the rest of what was needed. Is that enough? Yes. And no.

The Intentional Assistant Is God-Called

Yes. "The anger of the LORD burned against Moses" because Moses failed to believe that God's power was enough to make up for his own human flaws.

And no. God most likely never intended for Moses to stand alone (in the human sense). Even the Almighty does not act alone, but in concert with the other persons of the Trinity. He had already prepared Aaron for service with his brother and had already sent Aaron out to meet with Moses: "The anger of the LORD burned against Moses, and He said, 'Is there not your brother Aaron the Levite? I know that he speaks fluently. And moreover, behold, he is coming out to meet you; when he sees you, he will be glad in his heart'" (Exod. 4:14).

Aaron's speaking ability as well as his intimate knowledge of Moses' beginnings and God's saving work uniquely suited him to complement his brother in leadership. God knew that Moses needed an assistant. He not only knew it; he prepared for and provided it. His anger burned against Moses because Moses didn't understand that part of God being enough for Moses included God's provision of human assistance as well.

Senior pastors—and for that matter, assistant pastors—would do well to learn this lesson from Moses. God will not give you a challenge that you can conquer easily. You must know that if God called you to this position and this place, he will complete what he started in you—even if you feel inadequate for the task, even if he hasn't yet given you the assistant you feel you so desperately need, even if your congregation has only two members—and they're your mom and your dad. Do not insist that God should follow your timing.

Like Aaron for Moses, sometimes God gives us things that we want, ultimately to both our good and our detriment. He gives it to us when he was going to give it to us anyhow, but he just didn't want us to have to beg, cry, scream, and kick for it. It's no different than with our children. We probably would give them anything they want. We would probably give them the candy they wanted. But then they kicked and screamed for it. So now we give them the candy, but instead of giving it in the way we wanted, we hand it to them wanting to say, "Here it is! Eat this candy. I hope you suck it and get a sore tongue!"

God did give Moses an assistant through his anger, but he didn't choose angrily who it would be. With forethought and love, God prepared and called Aaron to a lifetime of serving as an assistant to Moses.

Assistants, Not Alternates

Assistant pastors are just as much God's priority as the primary leaders or senior pastors are. Did you hear that? Just as God prepared, called, and supported Moses, he prepared, called, and supported Aaron in the role he had chosen for him.

God Ordains the Job Description

And the Lord didn't stop there. Anticipating confusion in the duties of each, God clarified their job descriptions. He wanted Moses to perform in relationship to and through Aaron: "You are to speak to him and put the words in his mouth; and I, even I, will be with your mouth and his mouth, and I will teach you what you are to do. Moreover, he shall speak for you to the people; and it shall come about that he shall be as a mouth for you, and you shall be as God to him" (Exod. 4:15–16).

The duties and authority of each man were enumerated clearly by these words.

- God spoke to Moses.
- Moses spoke to Aaron.
- God taught Moses what to do and say.
- Aaron conveyed Moses' message to the people.
- God gave Moses instructions on how to use His power.

Because of this outline of duties, Moses and Aaron both understood what God intended.

And both Moses and Aaron were pleased with the process, as illustrated in Exodus 4:27: "Now the LORD said to Aaron, 'Go to meet Moses in the wilderness.' So he went and met him at the mountain of God, and he kissed him." Later as Moses and Aaron appeared before the congregation of Israel, God allowed them to perform before the people what God had planned—Moses the leader and Aaron the assistant, performing the will and call of God.

Made for Moses

In today's terminology, Aaron would be called an intentional assistant. Aaron never replaced Moses as primary leader. Instead, he complemented Moses. God did expand Aaron's role by appointing him to the priesthood, but he never elevated Aaron to Moses' role of leadership. God called Aaron to an assistant role—for a lifetime. Was there a time when Aaron bristled under the reality of being the second chair? Yes. Along with Miriam in Numbers 12, Aaron spoke out against Moses, questioning his authority and leadership: "Then Miriam and Aaron spoke against Moses because of the Cushite woman whom he had married (for he had married a Cushite woman); and they said, 'Has the LORD indeed spoken only through Moses? Has He not spoken through us as well?' And the LORD heard it" (Num. 12:1–2).

35

Aaron wanted a bit more of the limelight. He wanted some of the recognition that Moses was receiving. It's a natural human response, but in this case, a sinful one— jealousy. God responded quickly, reaffirming his choices for head leader and assistant: "Hear now My words: If there is a prophet among you, I, the LORD, shall make Myself known to him in a vision. I shall speak with him in a dream. Not so, with My servant Moses, he is faithful in all My household; with him I speak mouth to mouth, even openly, and not in dark sayings, and he beholds the form of the LORD. Why then were you not afraid to speak against My servant, against Moses?" (Num. 12:6–8).

The Lord had chosen to give Moses special privilege along with an awesome responsibility. And it's God's right as the sovereign Lord to make that choice. Every assistant struggling with the green-eyed monster, whether in terms of recognition, salary, or authority, should also remember that while every calling may not be equal in status, it is equal in importance for the fulfillment of God's plan. You never know, God might be planning to start a priesthood through your loyal service. If God has called you to an assistant role, stay the course.

The Unintentional Assistant

On the other hand, God calls some people to train for the pastorate through the assistant role. Using the assistant role as training for the senior pastorate should not diminish the position and make it "second fiddle." On the contrary, it emphasizes the importance of the assistant position and the close relationship that should exist between the two positions.

The fact that God finds the assistant role adequate for developing his head leaders should tell us that the job is not second best. Rather, the assistant role adds essential qualities and understanding to the character of future senior pastors, qualities that may not otherwise have come naturally. At the very least, the intern should gain an appreciation for the trials and challenges that his future assistants will face, making him better able to lead them. At the very best, by learning to submit to the senior pastor's authority, the intern will learn how to submit to God's leadership and vision—a crucial element for avoiding rashness and pride as the head leader.

Unlike Aaron, after serving Moses in various capacities, Joshua became the leader of Israel. His style and function were that of an intern or apprentice learning the fine details of leadership from Moses. Joshua was always a leader-in-training, even if he didn't know it. He was sitting in the brass section, but he was really a first violin learning two jobs.

Our first glimpse of Joshua is during a time in the wilderness when there was no established military. Moses groomed Joshua as the person who would lead the military into victory in their fight against the Amalekites. We are not told whether Moses spotted Joshua's leadership potential, or if God told Moses to select Joshua. Whatever the case, the Lord agreed with the choice and directed Moses to prepare Joshua: "Then the LORD said to Moses, 'Write this in a book as a memorial, and recite it to Joshua, that I will utterly blot out the memory of Amalek from under heaven'" (Exod. 17:14). Although Joshua did not fully understand God's plans at this point, it does appear that God had special plans for this young man as a person who would lead the people as Moses' successor.

Training with Intention

Where was God's perfect place to train the young man who would take over for Moses? At the very feet of the man he would replace—and as an assistant. In hindsight, we can see the perfection of Joshua's training for his future role. At the time, however, perhaps all Joshua could see was his desire to serve his godly leader faithfully.

Training with Intimacy

Joshua's assistantship was different than Aaron's. Aaron was eventually given charge over the priesthood and was given duties to accomplish separate from Moses. But Scripture reveals Joshua participating in intimate moments of training and service *with* Moses. One example occurred when Moses received the tablets of the law from the Lord: "So Moses arose with Joshua his servant, and Moses went up to the Mountain of God" (Exod. 24:13). Joshua is here identified as Moses' servant. And he was given the intimacy of being invited to the mountain of God while all others, including second-in-command Aaron, were given instructions to wait below.

Moses gave young Joshua hands-on mentoring. This theme recurs throughout Exodus. Joshua is pictured as one who was always available to Moses when needed. As his servant, he spoke, he shared, and he savored the moments he spent with Moses.

Quality Interns Serve Humbly

Joshua served Moses as an assistant for a long time. Numbers 11:28 describes Joshua as "the attendant of Moses from his youth." Forty years later, Joshua no longer was a young man, yet he continued to serve Moses well. Up until this point, Joshua had not been given any firm indication that he would one day be the "senior pastor." But Moses included Joshua in some of his most intimate moments with the Lord and gave him opportunity to test his wings. Still, Joshua continued to serve humbly.

That's a good assistant. A good assistant, even if he's an intern ready to take over leadership, should not force the issue. He should be the intern when God has him as the intern, and he should be the senior pastor when God has him as the senior pastor. Trying to be senior pastor when you're in the intern state doesn't work.

Consider Peter's internship under Jesus. The unintentional assistant will do well to avoid Peter's mistakes. Peter had the passion to lead as first chair, but it was not time for him to do so. He needed first to learn to submit to the vision of his mentor. He needed to learn endurance in faith to keep from sinking in the waves (Matt. 14:28–31). He needed to understand and accept the coming cross rather than rebuke Jesus for discussing it (Matt. 16:22–23). He needed to learn how to stand against the opposition rather than deny his salvation (Matt. 26:33–35, 69–75).

Peter had the makings of a great leader, but he tended to rush ahead of God and cut his own path. Eventually, Peter did learn how to lead by leaning on God's strength and wisdom, and Christ ushered him into the senior pastor position.

Practice Leads to Perfection

At Oak Cliff Bible Fellowship, we've had interns just waiting to get their own churches. They were already lining up how they were going to be different from our church. They didn't want to be bothered with us anymore; we were too liberal this way, too conservative that way. These leaders have had difficulties. And the difficulty they've had is *not* that they couldn't preach or teach. The difficulty they've had is dealing with the boards, committees, and task-oriented groups. They couldn't translate their theology into ministry. They might create a Bible study on a subject, but they hadn't spent enough time letting God shape their spiritual lives under the mentorship of another proven leader. The congregations they served saw these pastor's lives as being different than what they were teaching. The people read us more than they read the Bible. I found that to be the case almost all of the time.

The lesson for the unintentional assistant is to be the best intern you know to be. All the jobs that appear to be "below" you, go ahead and do them. As you learn from every situation, it will cause you to grow. Then, when you become a senior pastor, you'll realize the value of work. As you get the chance while you're an intern to attend board meetings, go to funerals, officiate at weddings, perform baptisms, learn the ordinances, and learn the constitution of the church, do so. Then you will be able under any circumstances to operate as a senior pastor from a realm of truth and experience rather than from a realm of make-believe or unpracticed theology.

God puts us in the incubators of internship for the purposes of learning in a real situation how the ministry looks. Think of all those things Joshua saw Moses handle during the forty-plus years in the wilderness. Think of the conversations they had in Moses' tent after Moses talked face-to-face with the Lord. Think of the impact Moses' one sin as leader had on Joshua. He was aware like no other that Moses' failure to obey God cost Moses the opportunity to enter the Promised Land.

Many future senior pastors have dreams of what their ministry will be like. It's going to be big, and everybody will hear them preach. A good internship can let us see that the reality of leadership is plain, old hard work. And the hard work is that you've got to be in the hospitals doing the hard visits. You've got to be discipling men and women when you didn't expect it. You've got to be doing the counseling of other people. It's not just about being a big shot and writing books about the ministry; it's actually performing ministry, and letting the book write itself from what you've been involved in through your life experiences.

Many of our interns who trained hard—and did the things we asked them to do—are great pastors. Even their wives had a clear image of what it meant to be a senior pastor's wife. They realized they were going to get some hard knocks every once in awhile. They weren't going to always be accepted. These men and their families had a clear vision, and they seemed ready to move into the senior pastor's role.

Leadership Transfer

So for about forty years—whether Joshua understood God's call for future leadership or not—he understood that God had placed him in an assistant role. He did not waste the time as being unimportant. Then, near the end of Moses' life, God commissioned Joshua:

> Then Moses spoke to the LORD, saying, "May the LORD, the God of the spirits of all flesh, appoint a man over the congregation, who will go out and come in before them, and who will lead them out and bring them in, that the congregation of the LORD may not be like sheep which have

no shepherd." So the LORD said to Moses, "Take
Joshua the son of Nun, a man in whom is the
Spirit, and lay your hand on him; and have him
stand before Eleazar the priest and before all the
congregation; and commission him in their sight.
And you shall put some of your authority on him,
in order that all the congregation of the sons of
Israel may obey him." (Num. 27:15–20)

God cared enough about his congregation not only to
prepare a new leader, but also to plan for a smooth transition. Requesting God's choice of appointment, Moses began
transferring the power and authority of Israel's leadership to
Joshua. This new leader had completed his internship with
passing grades. He was mentioned as having been filled
with the spirit of wisdom. Notice Joshua never asserted
himself as the next leader. He waited until he was called.
Moses laid his hands on him, and the people listened.

In Deuteronomy 34, Joshua's partial leadership became
full leadership upon Moses' death. A new era of leadership was ushered in under Joshua. The baton had been
passed. In Joshua 1, God exalted Joshua as the new leader
of all of Israel. This is a good picture of leadership transfer.
Knowing the importance of properly mentoring interns as
Moses seems to have known—valuing and building their
strengths rather than bogging them down with tedious
tasks—produces assistants who will serve God and their
congregations well.

The Unintentional Pastor

In the last chapter, I described this category of assistant pastors as men who failed in the senior pastorate and later realized that their gifts fit better as assistants. Over the years I've seen that as the main cause for this category. But sometimes the Lord has a more positive purpose and actually calls intentional assistants or men who should be intentional assistants to temporarily assume a senior pastor role. Such is the case in the New Testament with Barnabas. God did not view this man who was more comfortable in the second chair as second rate. Rather, he found Barnabas valuable not only for mentoring fledgling senior pastors but also for filling the void as senior pastor until his students were ready to take over.

Barnabas had a unique role in that he seems to have had gifts suitable to both the pastorate and the assistantship. His passion, however, lay in mentoring others.

In Acts 9, Barnabas was faithfully serving under the disciples in Jerusalem when Saul, or Paul, arrived on the scene. Barnabas immediately realized Paul's potential and began to encourage and intercede for him. Later, in Acts 11, the Jerusalem church found a need in Antioch and, finding Barnabas a match for the need, they sent him to pastor. He went and succeeded. But Barnabas also knew a better match than himself; he sought out Paul from Tarsus.

Although Paul had been preaching Christ boldly for a number of years by this time, God still had him in the assistant incubator stage. God used Barnabas to establish

Paul's credentials and to guide him into the fulfillment of all that God had planned for him. At the time when God needed Barnabas to lead, he led. At the time when God needed Barnabas to recede to second chair, Barnabas needed no extra prodding. And the text changes from recounting the acts of "Barnabas and Paul" to the acts of "Paul and Barnabas."

Barnabas's humble acceptance of his calling as assistant should encourage all pastors who find that continued ministry—for whatever reason—will mean accepting what is perceived by most people as a lesser role. Rather than worry about who had top billing, Barnabas desired to be used by God to reach others for Christ, in whatever position God placed him in. That humility led him to be instrumental in training Paul and John Mark, both of whom went on to surpass him in name, ministry, and recognition. Barnabas remained true to the Almighty's calling no matter where it led him. In doing so he brought little glory to himself but great glory to God.

God's Priority for the Assistant

It is clear in these models that God values the assistant position just as much as he values the senior pastorate. We've seen God taking the initiative with the Aaron/Moses relationship in making sure that the leader and his assistants understood their clearly defined roles. We've also found that just because a man fills an assistantship role does not mean that he is less spiritual or less wise than the senior pastor. After all, like Barnabas, he may have mentored that pastor. The main difference, then, between the positions of senior pastor and the assistant seems to be God's intentions and the unique gifts he has given to the people in these roles.

God does not view the senior pastor as better. Why should we? As in the teamwork of the Trinity, senior pastor and associates differ only positionally, not personally. Consider the description of the second chair in Hebrews 1:2–3: "[God] in these last days has spoken to us in His Son, whom He appointed heir of all things, through whom also He made the world. And He is the radiance of His glory and the exact representation of His nature, and upholds all things by the word of His power. When He had made purification of sins, He sat down at the right hand of the Majesty on high."

The Father honors the second chair by making Christ heir of all things, recognizing the Son's perfect work in the world's creation and salvation. Personally, the Son is the "exact representation" of the Father, not a lesser being. Yet, the Son still recognizes the Father's leadership. He does not usurp the Father's throne; he sits in the place of honor beside it. Although Christ was equal to God, he "did not regard equality with God a thing to be grasped" (Phil. 2:6). He accomplished the work assigned to him, and "He was faithful to Him who appointed Him" (Heb. 3:2a).

If you are an assistant or an associate pastor, are you being faithful to accomplish the work allotted to you? Do you even know what it is? If you are a senior pastor or board looking for a good assistant, do you know what to look for? How do you find that number-one man for the second spot, the man you can introduce with confidence saying, "This is my second chair, my chosen one. Listen to him"?

To start, you look at the way God designed him.

Chapter Three

Designed
for the Second Chair . . .
or for Concertmaster?
UNDERSTANDING YOUR CALLING

A man's gift makes room for him,
And brings him before great men.
(Prov. 18:16)

You know you're an assistant pastor if . . .

- you're called on to preach and you have something better to do;
- you're always in the last car when the church goes anywhere;
- your congregation doesn't know your full name; and
- the church member sitting next to you asks if this is your first time to attend the service.

We can joke about the associate pastor's lack of recognition among his congregation. Since he is not the top authority in the church, it is natural that the assistant pastor be somewhat forgotten. After all, if we ask the average person who won the NBA championship last year, he or she might know the answer. But if you ask that same person who came in second in those years, you'll most likely receive a blank stare. We can joke, but we need to recognize the problem. As congregations, as senior pastors, and even as assistants, we don't fully value the assistant's gifts and talents that he uses to serve the body. But just because the associate often accomplishes his work behind the scenes does not mean that we should esteem it any less than the senior pastor's preaching.

As Paul writes in 1 Corinthians:

> Now there are varieties of gifts, but the same
> Spirit. And there are varieties of ministries, and
> the same Lord. . . . If the whole body were an eye,
> where would the hearing be? If the whole were
> hearing, where would the sense of smell be? But
> now God has placed the members, each one of
> them, in the body, just as He desired. . . . And
> the eye cannot say to the hand, "I have no need of
> you"; or again the head to the feet, "I have no need
> of you." On the contrary, it is much truer that the
> members of the body which seem to be weaker are
> necessary. (1 Cor. 12:4–5, 17–18, 21–22)

We could all aspire to become the eyes of the body, the mouth, or the hands. Imagine if for every concert all the violin players had to fight it out on stage to determine who got to play the solos! Of course, that doesn't happen because the conductor has already chosen the concertmaster and designated him for that role—he has also appointed all the other members of the orchestra to play the supporting parts in the symphony.

Whether you are in the ministry, entering the ministry, or even examining some other aspect of your life, do you know how God designed you? Did he gift you for concertmaster? Or for second chair? At this point, I'm not asking you to think about what positions are available to you right now or even what position you think you want. I'm asking you to evaluate your temperament, skills, and gifts to discern which role fits you best.

Personality Types

Like the parts of the body, senior pastors and assistant pastors come in all shapes and sizes. There are no right or wrong gifts or personalities for senior pastors and associates, only tendencies. For instance, the classic personality types for senior pastors—if we rely on the DISC model originally proposed by William Marston in 1928—are the high "D," the determined, driven type like my senior pastor, Dr. Evans, and the high "I" personality, the interactive and influential types. The "S"—steady, serving behind-the-scenes—and

"C"—critical, detailed and law conscientious—personalities lean toward supportive roles.

I'm not saying that the "S" and "C" personalities could not be excellent senior pastors. However, especially at a larger church, unless the "S" and "C" types also exhibit strong "D" or "I" blends, the laid-back side of the "S" usually causes him to fade into the woodwork, while the precision of the "C" personality will overwhelm him as senior pastor. He will see too many areas that he will want to fix at one time.

Giftedness and Goals

How does your personality fit with your goals? Over your life experience, have you mainly found yourself in the leading position? Or has God given you many opportunities to learn to follow well? You might even consider your family history. Just as our bloodline comes down and we inherit certain diseases within our families—the men have a tendency toward heart trouble or the women suffer frequently from breast cancer—we also have the possibility of inheriting natural leadership or servant traits.

In my bloodline, it seems that both my mother and father were servant types. My brother also found joy and fulfillment as an assistant principal for much of his life. Perhaps the Hawkins bloodline creates great servants and assistants to the people. We don't mind being up front playing first violin, but we do well in the second chair.

Traits of Assistants

All pastors, of course, need a heart for God and for people, a compassion that will allow them first of all to hear and to heed God's call. The special nature of supporting a senior pastor, however, requires that the assistant and associate pastor also have certain other skills, gifts, and traits—qualities that go beyond knowing the specifics of assembling a Sunday school ministry or performing worship on Sunday morning.

Team Ability

Assistant pastors need to be able to enjoy the company of a group of people. As staff members, they will be working most of the time in committees, boards, and team situations.

Humility

They need to be humble and able to suffer the loss of higher pay, prestige, and earthly remembrance with grace. Although part of this book's argument is that associate pastors should be held in higher esteem, the reality remains that supportive personnel will not receive the same kudos as the out-front leader. Like Aaron to Moses, like children to their parents, like wives to their husbands, assistants have to learn to accept graciously God's choice of headship in their lives.

Loyalty and Obedience

Along with accepting that leadership, the assistant needs to exhibit loyalty and obedience so that the senior pastor-assistant relationship can function. A headstrong individual who strikes out on his own and who hasn't learned to bring his personality into line with someone else's ideas will flounder in the assistant position.

Patience

The assistant must cultivate patience and strong communication skills—not just the one-way communicating of preaching—but the interpersonal communication that will allow him to understand and connect with the senior pastor.[1]

A straw poll asking several senior pastors the top five qualities they valued most in their associates revealed these answers:

- Biblical soundness
- Loyalty
- Integrity
- Flexibility
- Pulpit ability
- Walking with God
- Commitment
- Servanthood
- Self-starter

- Competence
- Professionalism

Do these traits and qualities look like you?

Skills of the Assistant Pastor

An assistant also needs to be prepared in the following list of skills to serve in his position and meet the special needs of the congregation. He will be called upon to:

- manage the spiritual life of the church,
- motivate volunteers for ministering,
- aid congregations in understanding and using their gifts,
- disciple special needs,
- mentor young believers and leaders,
- spiritually advise the senior pastor, and
- organize and develop effective programs that fulfill the senior pastor's vision.

Living within Another's Vision

The assistant has the special responsibility to learn to live within the vision of the senior pastor and to translate that vision to make it work well for him, the congregation, and the rest of the people, even if he may at times personally disagree with it. This aspect of the staff role is so important that all aspiring assistants should have practical experience taking someone else's vision and making it work. You need to know how to sharpen it and retool it without changing it or discouraging it, and certainly not disparaging the vision of the pastor for the congregation.

Jack-of-All-Trades

The associate must also keep in mind that while you might be taking a position as worship director or education leader, if you minister well, you will also fulfill other roles. Gaining as many ministry skills as possible during training and schooling will be helpful. For example, as you develop a relationship with the people, you will always be counseling on some level whether you excel at counseling or not, because people trust you and want to talk to you. You will perform mediation and reconciliation frequently in your ministry. It's good to have experience in this area. And you will need to understand the financial administration of the church.

Traits of Senior Pastors

Senior pastors, on the other hand, are preachers and proclaimers. They have unquenchable passion for preaching and teaching. And they inspire followers with their leadership.

Passionate Visionaries

The senior pastor will be responsible for vision casting. Dr. Evans, my senior pastor, is a super visionary. Early on in our work together, he called me at three o'clock in the morning just to share the vision he'd had about what needed to be done. Not being the visionary myself, I said, "Couldn't this wait until eight? Or when I come into work?" But he was just popping with visions and could see the whole church in his mind, and he was anxious to tell somebody immediately. I knew then that God had absorbed him in the vision for this church.

On the flip side of that, when he finished telling me about it, I might say to him, "OK, now here's how it can work out in the church." I could complete his vision with the smaller specifics, including telling him which staff member could do it best.

Confident Decision Makers

The senior pastor will also need to be confident in leading. Whether he exhibits a shepherd style or a rancher style, he needs to be comfortable having the church and the staff constantly looking to him for the hard answers and decisions. He must also be able to feel comfortable and content set apart from everyone else because he will experience separation at the top.[2] The strong "D" personality handles these aspects the most naturally of each of the four types. The high "C" and "S" personalities, on the other hand, usually struggle to make fast, hard decisions as the senior pastor. (As a staff member, however, once the "C" has convinced himself or been convinced about the right course, he will cover your back, get it done, and make sure it's done right.)

As the headman, the senior pastor will have to come to terms with the phrase, "The buck stops here." I personally hate it when it's time to ask people for money. Dr. Evans, though, just says it's part of the job. "It's just something you have to do. Let's go." So while I'm cringing over in the corner, feeling as awkward as a Labrador pup trying to grow into his tremendous feet, Dr. Evans can always present his plan that he has laid out about money issues.

Pragmatic Delegators

As a senior pastor's church grows larger, he will also need to be able to let go of some of the one-on-one ministry in favor of overseeing the church as a whole. This can be especially difficult for those pastors with a shepherding style (often the style of the "I" personality), where the senior pastor treasures the ministry of his people on an individual basis. For him, counseling, hospital calls, and personal lunches are more enjoyable than task-oriented or administration duties, and, to some extent, even sermon preparation. He can keep that one-on-one ministry with his staff—and he should—but he won't be able to keep all those relationships with the entire congregation.

One of the biggest transitions of growing from about two hundred members to the five hundred to one thousand mark is that the pastor has to have a change of mind. Now he has to be able to say, "I've got to let go of other things that I used to do personally and give them to someone else to accomplish—and I've got to trust him to get those things done."

Before, where a song leader just guided the music suggested by the pastor, now the church has a worship leader who ties together how the music flows and the kind of topics or themes the service will have—someone who can really determine what theological truths he wants to teach through the music. So now the church moves from just singing to developing a theology about worship. That cannot come without study in this area and thinking about it on an every day, every moment basis. Then singing transforms itself. It changes from a choir to a worship center. That shift has to happen.

The pastor has to recognize that though he's been expert in a lot of areas, now he's not expert in every area like he used to be. There's a new man or new woman in town who has expertise in an area he is not up to speed in. And this sometimes is a point of friction. Can the senior pastor let go? Can he deal with the member who says, "I always used to talk with you about Sunday school issues; why is the associate the go-between now?" Can he connect with his congregation without always being the one to lay hands on them in time of need?

At Oak Cliff Bible Fellowship, Dr. Evans's vision was so enormous that it carried out and beyond the church in many cases. It's what started the Urban Alternative. His vision was not only for the church but also for the nation. When we started together, vision was not a part of my role, and God did not gift me with any. Over the years—about when we reached one thousand to twelve hundred in membership—my ability to develop a vision within his vision evolved so much that not only could I start almost previsioning what he was about to say or do, but God also started giving me visions on the aspects of the church that I had to take care of—on how it would grow.

We had reached a different level, and Dr. Evans even had to release some of his hold on creating the vision for our church because God had given him so much responsibility in that area.

Complementing Each Other

I've tried to present some of the qualities that must be present for the assistant to remain satisfied and the qualities that will aid the senior pastor in his responsibilities. These are those things that both assistants and senior pastors need to be able to consider for their role and say, "That's me," or, "There's no way I could live under those restrictions." But the most important aspects of looking at personality types and giftedness, beyond discerning trends, are making sure that the assistant is gifted for the particular needs of the position and understanding that a senior pastor should not surround himself with staff members like himself.

For example, a task-oriented man ("D" or "C" personalities) should team with more people-oriented personalities ("I" and "S"). A "D" who leads with a more domineering style might look for the quiet influence of an "S" personality with the gift of leadership. An "I" personality needs to make sure that he has staff members with a knack for meeting deadlines.

We also lead according to our giftedness. A strong evangelist needs to maintain equilibrium with someone who is good at discipling and teaching or administration. The man highly gifted in leadership or apostleship might want to make sure he listens to a wise and discerning associate. The combinations can be endless, but the staff *should* exist in combination rather than as clones of one another in order to serve the body well.[3]

Know Yourself

When I studied psychology in undergraduate school, I had one professor who stated that he wanted us to know more about ourselves than anyone else. He expected us at least to be aware of our own personal drives. Every minister needs to do the same. He needs to understand himself as well as the position he desires. Personality tests and work inventories abound. Although tests and inventories cannot measure everything, they can expose a lot. Assistants must know what they really want and be honest about tendencies they have developed in the ministry. Only then can they look at a potential placement and see whether they are going to be able to complement the senior pastor and staff.

As I've mentioned, early on in my ministry, I thought I wanted to be a senior pastor. I could see myself being a pastor, except . . . I thought about the discipline of putting sermons together every week, and I didn't want that pressure. I didn't mind preparing sermons and doing some administrative chores on the side, but I didn't feel like I wanted the problem of preaching every Sunday and going to the text and having to work it out—especially after I finished my training at Dallas Seminary when I realized how much work this was. This just wasn't my passion.

I did, however, want to touch people in many different ways. I knew how to do programming for the church that worked. And I knew how to disciple and care for people.

Designed for Teamwork

I learned that my gifts were with people. Dr. Evans can exegete Scripture with the best of them, but when we get together, I know the people. I know how to exegete them in terms of their needs, wants, and expectations. I could exegete how the people would handle his messages, even the Scripture text itself—how the people would respond to it, and even how they *should* respond to it. And I was able to create programs and environments that gave his sermons even more impact. I listened to the things he said, and I would say, "Perhaps we need something like you preached about this past Sunday."

Part of your design—like Aaron to Moses—has a direct relationship to the person or church with whom God is calling you to work. If you are to be an assistant, God is calling you to be a specific person's assistant for a specific purpose and a specific time. God designed me to fit with Dr. Evans's style of senior pastoring and leadership, to complement him and make him the best pastor he can be.

He is a fabulous senior pastor, but for all his gifts and skills, he is only one person. He can't meet all the needs of a congregation our size. Truly, even if the congregation were smaller, he still wouldn't be all things to all people. He is gifted for what God has called him to do, and I am gifted for the work God has for me. From time to time, I've had people mention their appreciation because I took time with them, and I looked them in the eye, and I shook their hand. But for Dr. Evans, sometimes people didn't feel that connection with him because he might walk past them and not speak, being so focused on his task. God created him to be task oriented, always looking at what he needs to do as opposed to what he does.

We're like two bookends. On one end, he can rightly divide the exact Word of God. On the other end, I can let you see how it's lived in the experience of the people. So I had a lot of people assignments that weren't necessarily in my job description simply because I was better at working with some people groups than he might have been.

The Call

When it comes to the bottom line, however, no matter which personality type you are, the key to knowing your next step is understanding your call. Seeking church after church for job placement does not answer this issue. Search committees and senior administration will have less knowledge on this than you. An assistant, whether intentional or unintentional, can be complete only when he realizes his position originates with God and not the senior pastor or the congregation. The issue then becomes what is "calling," and how do I know I have one? A calling is an individual divine passion to be led of God and to know him through his leading. It requires a person to recognize with certainty that God has a larger purpose for his life. God then chooses to fulfill an individual's calling by drafting that person to play a specific part in his divine plan.

God's calling upon a life is different for each individual, yet is actualized through depending on the Lord to reveal what it is he or she needs to become. "Before I formed you in the womb I knew you, and before you were born I consecrated you; I have appointed you a prophet to the nations" (Jer. 1:5). As illustrated in this verse, a person's calling may be determined before birth. It then develops over time as he grows through various phases of his life. It is given and clarified only by God. One's calling can only be achieved in God's appointed time, and both negative and positive experiences are intentional parts of it.

When a person is fulfilling his calling, he finds that it requires less and less hard work by the flesh and more and more faith and trust in Christ. For the pastor, the specific and special separation into the ministry is an awesome privilege. It must not be cheapened by the attitude that one is being hired for a job but that one is partaking as an heir in God's kingdom. For the assistant, the opportunity to help the senior pastor lead the congregation to salvation and to discovering their own calling and passion of life should be overwhelming.

But how do I know the specifics of my call? God may make your calling as clear as Moses and Aaron's. He speaks from a burning bush and sears the message into your soul. For others, like me, understanding your specific calling takes much prayer, fasting, and waiting upon the Lord. You can help the process along, however, by taking stock of how God has designed you.

The Job: Bigger than You

Kevin Lawson performed a study in 1997 of the associate pastor's ability to survive and thrive in his role. Based on his survey of 418 associate ministers across denominational lines, the factor most selected as affecting associate staff longevity and satisfaction in ministry was "a sense of fulfillment that comes from using my gifts/abilities in this way."[4] When the intentional assistant or the senior pastor-turned-assistant realizes his design *and* fulfills that call, he finds it the best place possible on this earth.

But what about the unintentional assistant? How do you fulfill your role as assistant when your giftedness is leading you toward the pastorate? You have to remember that your calling is bigger than you. It's not only what benefit you're going to get out of it; it's bigger than that. You're being called to the kingdom of God in a particular place, and you have to perform to the best of your ability. As opposed to just seeing your job as a stepping-stone, God wants you to step on that stone in the right way. Even if it's a step to the next ministry, you must glorify God by your good work.

Those people who say, "Since I'm going on to the next church, I don't really have to get involved here; I don't have to know what the pastor is thinking," are being shortsighted. They don't learn what God has for them to learn in that place. They may go out and fail because they didn't develop the skills they needed when they had the opportunity.

Instead of their short-sighted approach, they should develop a good work ethic and a good dialogue with the senior pastor. They should learn what his vision is and learn how to keep that vision intact with the people he serves. They need to figure out how they can bring their own giftedness under the service of the church and the pastor. That's the bigger picture. The unintentional assistant needs to ask himself, "How can I help move this congregation to create the kingdom of God in this time and in this area?"

If the unintentional assistant can't fulfill that mission as an assistant, he needs to move on. He needs to find another church or move into the pastorate right then. But beware. Some interns have a stubbornness that says, "I know what I'm doing because I've been to seminary." Sometimes it takes failing in a pastorate position to knock this stubbornness out of a man . . . and the congregation suffers because of it.

If you are an unintentional assistant who finds you have to constantly reign in your giftedness, pray. And then fall on your knees and pray again. Ask the Lord what he has for you to learn, and then get after learning it. Prepare yourself for the position he is preparing for you. Pray about it. Pray, do your job well, and wait. And when the Lord whispers to your heart that he has a new job for you to do, take it and fly. In the meantime, you can alleviate some of the discomfort by being open about your giftedness and needs when you interview and by taking the time to pursue a well-written job description.

Chapter Four

Knowing the Score:
Writing a Job Description

*You are to speak to him and put the words in his mouth
and I, even I, will be with your mouth, and his mouth,
and I will teach you what you are to do. Moreover, he shall
speak for you to the people; and it shall come about that
he shall be as a mouth for you, and you shall be as God
to him. (Exod. 4:15–16)*

What is a <u>job description</u>? A job description is a document that clarifies for both the hiring party and the one hired
what is expected of him, what compensation and benefits he
expects in return, and the various details that will make the
work relationship run smoothly.

An orchestra is never expected to play without first
being given the composer's score. Each player must learn
the notes and the timing designated in the music. Only

after the musician knows those boundaries can he add personality and flair to the composition. An assistant, too, should never be expected to perform his job without an adequate, written job description.

His job will inevitably extend beyond the written document, since no job description can capture every nuance of his ministry. Fitting in with a team's work habits, traditions, and personalities takes more than understanding one's expected duties; it takes sitting side by side with the other musicians, feeling the pulse of the music, the crescendo of emotion, and the flow of the musical phrases. At times, the associate will have to rely on his intuition to not only function well with the church staff, but to minister seamlessly with them. But the assistant will not be able to immerse himself in discovering these issues without first knowing which notes to play.

It's a Necessity!

Just as the Lord spelled out the individual roles for Moses and Aaron, associate and senior pastors need a foundation on which they can base their expectations of each other. The job description is perhaps the most important aspect of solid church growth. When the roles of the senior pastor and assistant are well defined, everyone benefits from these relationships, especially the assistant who can only do his work well when he understands how the senior pastor wants support.

What happens without a good, clear outline? Does the staff have more freedom to pursue their goals? Far from it. Instead, the associate will find that the staff relationships weave into chaos and every job will be his—from picking up food at the store to setting up chairs in a room. He'll have no time left to do the ministry to which God has called him.

Or worse yet, without a job description, the pastor and associate might differ in their expectations and could have opposing viewpoints. One pastor I know had a volunteer assistant, but they weren't playing the same music. Discord between them occurred often. Then the pastor hired the man part-time, thinking the problem would get better. It didn't. Why? Because no one ever gave that innocent assistant the right music. They never cleared up the job description.

Sometimes, too, the pastor wants more than the assistant can handle. Or sometimes, the associate's expectation is so heavy the pastor feels the assistant infringing on his territory. The job description should answer these questions: When do I have the authority to not only review but to act? When can I act independently? And when do I act as a team? It should also answer: When I have the authority to make my own decisions about an issue, do I then report it as something I did with no questions asked? Or do I report it as asking permission?

That's a big rub. Because some things you do, you think you've done it, and you've done it right. Then the pastor says, "Oooh. That's not what I would have done. I want to change something." Then changing can be embarrassing and humiliating.

At the same time, realize that the job description is an intention of what you hope will happen, but it is not an indicator of what will always happen. Do you hear what I mean? It's what would happen on your best day when you look at everything running just right; that's what the job description answers. But it doesn't answer all the related things that you will have to perform. There will always be some things not in the job description, but if you don't do them, you'll be lost. In other words, the job description outlines the basics of your ministry so that *it* doesn't get lost. But you'll probably do a lot more than that; very rarely will you do less.

Applying Your Design

The job description will be key for many things, but especially for evaluating potential job placement. A really good description will help you know if your design fits at that church and with the senior pastor.

For example, let's say that you're an assistant pastor type, but you have a gift for creating visions. Or perhaps you are an unintentional assistant wanting more training in a certain area like working with church governing boards. Both of these persons might want to seek a position where the senior pastor gives more latitude to the staff for creating the vision of the church. Even still, you must find out whether the pastor is saying, "Create a vision and bring it to me to evaluate," or "Create a vision and act on it." The job description should both help clarify that issue and establish the lines of authority. If the description doesn't mention this issue, you will need to bring it up and negotiate it before you accept the position.

Unless you are a very unusual person, no position will include only those tasks for which you have a passion while leaving out those you don't prefer. But if you evaluate the job description carefully and negotiate it well, you should end up with enough emphasis on the ministry tasks for which you feel gifted and driven—and enough time slated into your schedule to complete them. Then all those other assignments will be easier to bear.

Points to Include

Whose responsibility is it to prepare the assistant's job description? This will vary from church to church. The senior administration will want a say in it, of course. But in order for the assistant to support the senior pastor, the senior pastor must have the latitude to specify what he needs from this staff member.

Senior pastors can become very impatient with pastoral staff that must be guided in every detail, especially as the relationships and knowledge of the job situations increase. They can alleviate much of this frustration by taking the time before interviewing and hiring to perfect each task detail of the assistant's job description. Of course, at a small church the assistant is a catchall position. But eventually it will become more refined, and you'll need to write it out. When you do, be sure to include the following:

Scope of the Position

Smaller churches must often select staff members who are generalists. Budget and congregational restraints limit their selection. But at larger churches, senior pastors, boards, and congregations must concern themselves with the specific ministries the associate pastor will oversee. Specialized ministry areas—worship pastors, youth ministers, Christian education and adult ministries, outreach pastors, counselors, and executive administrative assistants—all require specific and well-honed skills. Worship assistants must be able to minister quality music to all areas of the congregation, from youth to senior adult ministries. Youth ministers need to blend major youth segments to bring about one concerted movement. Executive assistants should be aware of church law and responsibilities of ministries with respect to the maintenance and scheduling of major church events. And adult ministry personnel must know how to lead everyone, from the newest believer to trained ministers.

Here, it becomes more obvious when an assistant pastor is ill equipped or emotionally unprepared to accept the challenge presented by the job description. Robert Radcliffe writes, "A problem may arise if aspiring associates have only observed one (solo) pastor in a church and have little or no acquaintance with anyone who ever served in the associate position."[1] Such can be the case when coming from smaller churches and the assistant pastor is expected to perform roles in larger churches that he has not observed. In such cases, the urgency intensifies for the assistant to be honest about what he or she is able or unable to perform.

When I started at Oak Cliff Bible Fellowship, I had to do a little of everything. I even directed the music for the church. I didn't major in music, though I could carry a tune, but that was a part of my role because nobody else was there to coordinate the music at the time, and we wanted one of the pastoral staff to lead the music. Later that job shifted to a pastor of worship. (But I've never thought that our worship pastors have had as much fun with the job as I did. And I *know* the choir misses my windshield-wiper conducting!)

I also had to fill the role of director of Christian education for awhile. Even though I was the assistant pastor, we needed to develop how we were going to train our children, our youth, and our adults. So I put some programs together. Especially at the smaller church, the assistant will have a variety of jobs; he will have to do a little of everything, including building maintenance. I found myself doing that. Sometimes I went to train, and the room was set up, but we wanted the chairs rearranged differently to create the right environment. Now I could have let my ego get in the way and sat there and complained to my group about how that wasn't set up properly. I could have said, "That's not in my contract, let me call building maintenance," but by the time I called them and they arrived, I could have already done the job.

The question shouldn't be: Is this in my job description? The question should be: What's the best way to get this accomplished? And that's how it should be no matter if the issue is a minor one of chair arrangement or a more serious matter with spiritual impact. But if you don't first outline your scope of duties in the job description, you will be setting up the chairs wherever you go. And you won't know when you're interfering with someone else's job. If you do have set-up people or building maintenance, and you never let them work, you're not delegating authority. You're taking over someone else's job when you could be spending that time praying with a person before the meeting.

For the unintentional assistant, especially, evaluating and negotiating the scope of the position will help you determine whether you'll be receiving the right kind of experience. Don't forget—you will need the experience of the assistant role, too! But you also want to make sure you'll have many opportunities to preach and test your wings in other areas.

Required Training

A hiring church will of course make itself clear on the issue of expected training. These days, employment advertising reveals that many larger churches want trained, experienced seminarians to be on their staff. They want more training of a strict biblical nature to help the assistant understand the complexity of pastoring in the local church. Therefore, attendance at seminaries has increased.

But even with a Bible institute or seminary degree, interviewees still have difficulty determining if they are qualified for a position. Sometimes churches base qualifications on experience in the ministry. A new approach in our institutions of higher learning using a spiritual and experiential model to prepare assistants for the challenges of this millennium would greatly ease this problem. Pure academics and theological and biblical training are not enough to aid in the staffing of emerging megachurches. Bible institutes, Bible colleges, and seminaries need to prepare their students for the new issues of effective leadership training—for the pastoral support team as well as the senior pastor.

But churches can't wait for this new approach to occur. Senior pastors should expect that their associates will need training. Christ taught the disciples as they went, while they were entering the synagogues or the temple, or just walking from town to town. He said things like, "Look at that little widow over there; she's the one giving the real money." Assistants should always be open to learning. Some of the best lessons you'll learn about the ministry will be right in life—while a person is being funeralized or while a sermon is being delivered. And sometimes the best-fitting assistant for a position learned his ministry under the tutelage of his pastor.

Salary and Benefits

It's critical to know not only what you're going to be earning in the position but how much you really need to make. That's a different question than just what the salary is. The salary should answer the question, how can I minister to my wife and children with the amount of money that I have without needing to earn extra income? So although the average salary for that job in a given area may be only $15,000, you might say, "To truly do the job I need $25,000, because when I figure out my family's basic needs without trying to be extravagant, that's the number I come up with." You need to start the discussion from that frame of reference as opposed to coming back to them saying, "I need a raise, or I have to quit."

Talk up front so they can see your needs. The assistant especially needs to have a plan for his money needs. It's not begging for money for money's sake, but "I've got a daughter who's going to college in a couple years, and I've got to save," or "I have some bills that need to be met from when I was at another church. These bills need to be paid; otherwise I have a bad testimony." You need to negotiate on these points early on because that may help you make the decision to take or turn down the job. It should never be the final or most important reason for your decision, but it can help you make it.

Find out, too, the personnel policy requirements of the church. Understand the dress code. Understand your options for travel—is it included? How do you apply? Is it just given to you? Do you have to earn it? Do you have to send in a voucher? What are the expected working hours? Is there such a thing as "comp time"? Paid or unpaid? What are the vacation benefits? How does health insurance fit into the package? Knowing all these details ahead of time prevents distraction later from the true issue—ministry.

Preaching Responsibilities

Some assistants love to minister and hate to preach. On the other hand, some guys say, "Please let me preach, not every week, but occasionally." Each associate must examine his own desire for preaching. Then you need to find how much you can (or must) preach in the church, and how much you can preach outside the church. (This is also a negotiating point for supplementing your income.) Be sure to ask, do I lose money if I miss on Sunday? Is it frowned upon that I'm away on Sundays? What Sundays—and how many Sundays—do I get to preach and develop my own ministry and preaching?

This point should include a basic schedule of the time you'll have for both. Without it, you may discover that the only time you're allowed to preach is while you're on vacation. Preaching and ministry time and vacation time should be two separate times. You really shouldn't have to use your vacation time to preach elsewhere. Make sure you cover that point.

Board, Committee, and Congregational Responsibilities

The job description should explain (1) whether you are required to be *on* the elder board, and (2) whether you are required to be *at* the elder board meetings. We opted for both— that associates be on the elder board and attend meetings.

In the early years of Oak Cliff Bible Fellowship, I was the chairman of the elder board. I set the agenda and called for votes because we thought Dr. Evans shouldn't be responsible for such things. At the time we decided that the board should be separate from him. It was a lot of work, but I knew it was a part of my job.

About eight years later, we came to the conclusion that maybe the board needed him. The board was responsible to try to follow Dr. Evans's vision. So why not let him chair the board and let the rest of the people give votes? So we changed. And there are advantages and disadvantages of going both ways.

First, there is the time factor. Board meetings take time. Preparing for meetings takes time (at least it should if you're doing it right!). Not having to attend or plan the meeting frees you up for other ministry. But being a part of the meeting gives you more say over what your ministry will look like. There are other issues, too, such as will you be able to handle the awkwardness of helping to set the senior pastor's salary?

You also need to know in advance what other meetings and administration tasks you will lead. Taking on a job with high administration responsibilities when that is clearly not one of your gifts or skills will only frustrate you. On the other hand, these skills can be learned. You will need to know how to set clear agendas and know agenda planning for any meeting that you chair. After you set the agenda, make sure you can cover it in one meeting—and then do it. You might do more—good for you—but you must get at least that much done. And make sure you've given yourself time to be prepared. By being prepared, I mean having the main thinking and planning done, so those people who are coming in as volunteers can go to work as opposed to thinking through a lot of issues.

Hierarchy of Staff and Mediation

At Oak Cliff Bible Fellowship, I was next in line and did much more internally than the associate pastors. Because of the system we have now, when you say assistant pastor at our church, it's one person. And that one person is next in line to the pastor. You have Dr. Evans, then the assistant pastor, and then the associates. I had responsibilities directly over the other associates, and I had the final say when Dr. Evans was away. That's the positional hierarchy as it works at our church.

But nationwide, the role of the assistant at best is ambiguous. Some have responsibility for full-time staff. Others have responsibilities over areas without staff. Some have decision-making ability in the pastor's absence. Still others must check with the senior pastor for all authority issues. The job description must clarify these relationships with both the general and ministerial staff *before* conflict arises.

Human reality, even among pastors, means that all too often an appropriate positional hierarchy turns quickly into an unwritten pecking order. Tenure longevity, favoritism, and the size of a particular associate's budget can change how the senior pastor treats individual staff, and how the staff interacts with one another. Egos, emotions, and expectations get in the way of listening to the Lord's leading as a unified team.

Let me just say right now, let's not do that. These kinds of systems divide the staff and the church, especially in regard to the mutual respect needed by assistants for one another. Often when these unwritten rules get out of hand, they cause more confusion than unity. Such expressions of competitiveness damage both the internal and external witness of the local church.

The Godhead coreigns, coacts, and coserves in love. We must, as specially called shepherds of the church, exemplify that same model. How can we guide the church if through petty politics and pride we walk in the darkness? "The one who says he is in the light and yet hates his brother is in the darkness until now. The one who loves his brother abides in the light and there is no cause for stumbling in him. But the one who hates his brother is in the darkness and walks in the darkness, and does not know where he is going because the darkness has blinded his eyes" (1 John 2:9–11).

The amount of love or lack of it shared among believers toward a person ultimately influences how that person is regarded outside the church. We must demonstrate our love both within and without the body of Christ. Competition among assistants in programming, budgeting, and other areas is *not* OK. It's unbiblical.

Human failing and church politics are very real. We can accept that everyone will fail in this area, but we should not accept such failure as our standard. Love is the only positive approach to such a problem. Adhering to the principle of love, the pastoral staff needs to work at developing a biblical intimacy in the care of one another. Respect the wisdom that the long-term associate can lend on local issues. Respect the daily pressure and needs of the associate who is managing a larger budget. Respect the fresh ideas and energy of the newest members of the team. Assistants need to demonstrate a cooperative caring spirit with their peers. Senior pastors should lead and encourage this among their staffs. Meetings, fellowship times, and everyday work should reveal a caring attitude on a daily basis.

Ministering to the multiple needs of one another looms very high in creating a climate of cooperation. Therefore in a spirit of love, develop an appropriate positional hierarchy, so that when the senior pastor has to be away, or is unavailable, work can get done. Make sure everyone knows the policy for handling problems—to whom and when they should be taken. And then follow it.

Accountability and Evaluations

Good job descriptions help at evaluation time. It becomes an objective standard to which everyone can compare what you have accomplished.

Because I headed much of the leadership of our church, I was responsible for evaluations too. So I set up an evaluation tool with a measurement for all leadership in our church. Each year we have a chance to evaluate whether each person lived up to what he said he should or would live up to. It helps us hold our elders and deacons accountable. It helps us hold one another accountable. A clear, written description lets both the employee and the supervisor monitor progress throughout the year, and it eliminates surprises.

Expectations for Future Ministry Roles

Ministry changes as needs change. Most of the time, change occurs as life happens, but sometimes the change is known ahead of time. If you are expecting that your position will train you for further responsibility within the church, you need to make sure the possibility exists for an expansion of your duties. At the same time, you should find out if the staff is expecting you to take on an expanded role after you have settled into the church for, say, a year.

We had one associate who didn't realize he was going to be put in charge of finances. When he found out, he was overwhelmed. It's a lot of work, and not everyone has the skills and talent for the job. He had to address the issue with the leadership of the church as soon as he found out.

Administrative and Supervisory Responsibilities

Know in advance what latitude you will have in hiring helpers. Will you be in a supervisory role?

Sometimes this category can help the assistant who feels his job bridges the span between senior pastor and assistant. At a larger church, often the associate will manage his own staff and in many ways function as the "senior pastor" in his own area. Deliberately looking for a position that serves the senior pastor and is first chair for your own interests can become the best of both worlds if it fits your design.

Required Event and Meeting Attendance

And, of course, a job description that lists regularly scheduled meetings, events, and teaching duties that the assistant must attend will go a long way toward helping him estimate what his schedule will look like, so he can plan accordingly.

Further Questions to Ask

The following are some other questions that you might like to clarify during the interview process:

1. What is your expectation about the position? Share some of your strengths and fears about the position.
2. In what role do you view yourself? Intentional assistant, unintentional assistant, or unintentional pastor returning to an assistant position?
3. What is your relationship expectation of senior pastoral care? What issues about the senior pastor or congregation could frustrate you?
4. What are the lines of authority? When those lines are not present, what is expected of you?
5. What limitations do you see on yourself resulting from taking this position?
6. What rights do you have to your written materials that are produced by you for and through the church?
7. What unexpected issues might you face?
8. What is the standard of excellence that this church demands on teaching, preaching, and on written communication?

9. Be honest about issues being raised in the interview that might pose conflict for yourself or family.

10. Know what the congregation feels about your position. Know whether they accept it as a legitimate need.

Flexibility

The job description remains a living document, changing with the needs of the church and the growth of the assistant's abilities. In reality, it takes self-starting assistants and wisdom to know when to improvise for the overall good of the senior pastor and church congregation. Still, everyone must maintain a balance between what is written and unwritten, or the document will become worthless.

The assistant pastor must be aware of the varied needs of the church and senior pastor and respond in a supportive manner. Over the years, I had to continuously train to prepare for new ministry areas like church mediation and developing a financial plan to meet the needs of those who are struggling within the body. And every time we changed or grew new ministries, we had to find or create new biblically based materials to accompany it.

Sometimes your role changes in an instant: you have to put on your business suit because you've got to fire or replace staff, or, perhaps, all of a sudden you're in charge of acquiring the land for the new building project, as I was. Other times, you'll have to put on your judge's robe and mediate conflict, and you'll be expected to know the law concerning the church. Or perhaps you'll need your assistant principal's ruler to handle discipline issues or your chauffeur's hat to drive someone around and help him find a job. The ability to remain flexible will serve every assistant well.

The job description must remain open-ended enough to say, "And all the other duties that seem to commiserate with your position." Both sides need to understand that it's a fluid job description, that it is no hard and fast thing. In the ministry, you're going to handle a lot. Ultimately, the Lord has us in the associate's position to take the weight off the pastor. That's what a staff is all about. But on the other extreme, you need some parameters so you don't have to run out and do every little thing. And if the pastor does shove something outside your description onto you, you need to have permission to pass it on occasionally as well—give it to somebody else.

Just as each job description will be unique because the parties involved are uniquely gifted people, the job description will need repeated revamping as the dynamics of the ministry change. Over time you must continually renegotiate the document to keep it in line with reality and as a basis for working out new issues. In twenty-nine years, my job description often was transformed. It was always in transition. To the day we die it will be in transition because it changes for us from one period to the next. It changes even from one week to the next.

On every level of the church I could have said, "My job description requires me to do only these few things." But it would have been a mistake and a problem for the church. I had to be fluid enough to say my job description required me to do several things, and while these other tasks were beyond what was expected, we had to do them to get the job done. And I was the one to do them.

You must be able to adjust and readjust—do things on the move. At our church, ministry moves at a fast clip. Instead of waiting for things to calm down, you have to think on the move. You have to keep moving with the pace and slow it down when you can. Most of our decision making is done in movement. We've already got something going while we're writing something else to remodel it and reshape it.

Unpaid Staff

For those of you in smaller churches who are thinking, *We don't need to write job descriptions yet; we just have to do whatever comes up; we are the catchall pastors,* I have news for you. You have plenty of reasons to write job descriptions. You call them volunteers. I call them unpaid staff.

Job descriptions aren't needed just for full-time staff. They can also solve many of the misunderstandings between the leadership and unpaid staff by placing a limit on hours and responsibilities. At the same time, they verify exactly what is needed from each contributor. As far as I'm concerned, we should write job description for *every* position, whether paid or volunteer.

Volunteers and unpaid staff provide a large portion of the work of the church. Without them, we could never accomplish the ministry. We should respect and appreciate their efforts to multiply what the paid staff can accomplish, and their doing so without concern for compensation. These people serve out of love for the Lord. Let's not beat them up or string them along by asking them to fulfill ambiguous tasks with indefinite deadlines.

When people want to involve themselves in the church, you need to give them something tangible to do and expect them to do it. So whether you have two people in your church or two thousand, you need to make clear what your expectations are. You may not even be full-time paid yourself. Just as you need help so you don't have to work full-time for part-time pay, volunteers need boundaries so they can both feel like they've accomplished their job and not feel like they have been indentured as muzzled oxen (1 Tim. 5:18).

One of the reasons why we get the ebb and flow in people coming to our churches and then leaving is because we treat them like full-time paid staff when they should be treated like part-time staff or unpaid staff. We *should* say, "Here's your own job. Do the outreach program for me." But we also have to say, "Since I know you're an unpaid staff member, a volunteer, I'm going to limit what you do to three hours a week as opposed to what somebody else might do—and here are my priorities for what needs to be done." Then make sure you appreciate their efforts. That's good leadership.

A Two-Sided Coin

Job descriptions are vital to the process of ministering. Preset boundaries and expectations can help alleviate misunderstanding and allow the team to model the close-knit relationships of the Trinity. The description benefits the associate, allowing him to match his design to a position, to interpret how he can best fulfill his ministry passion, and to protect himself and his family from overwork. The description mostly answers the question from the bottom up. How will the assistant support the senior pastor? But the coin has two sides. For the role of the assistant to rise to peak effectiveness in our churches, we must also ask the question from the top down. How will the senior pastor support the assistant?

Chapter Five

Maintaining the Orchestra: Caring for the Assistant

Do nothing from selfishness or empty conceit, but with humility of mind let each of you regard one another as more important than himself; do not merely look out for your own personal interests, but also for the interests of others. (Phil. 2:3–4)

Let me take a moment to address the associate pastor role from another angle. As a senior pastor or as church leadership, how do you know it's time to hire an assistant? How do you choose the right one? And how do you care for that assistant so he can contribute to a fruitful ministry? I'd like to suggest that much of the current practices in multiplying staff fails to accomplish what we intend.

Deciding to Hire

What if I were to say . . .

I think every young man who has completed his education should immediately marry a young woman fresh out of high school. It really doesn't matter if he has found employment or living arrangements yet. His focus should be on finding an attractive, energetic woman who can take over the tasks of cooking, cleaning, and laundry for him. After all, he'll be too busy for those sorts of things.

If after a few years she leaves the marriage, the man should not feel shame or remorse. It happens quite frequently as the young wife experiences a lack of security, a lack of appreciation, and a lack of purposeful intention for her life other than playing housemaid. These things are often a part of marriage although her parents have probably filled her head with other dreams. Truly, at her tender age, she just doesn't have the maturity to endure the shattering of her illusions about marriage, and the husband can excuse the divorce because of his wife's inability to adapt.

But because he still needs household tasks taken care of, the man should immediately seek another wife. This time, he might try his luck with an older woman who has more experience in household management. Because he will be younger than she, he should not expect to include her in his outings with friends or in his hobbies—she would most likely be bored, anyway. He won't need to clear out any space for her things or give her room in his closets. And, if the budget is tight, he shouldn't feel the need to include her household needs in it. She has taken care of houses before and should be able to rely on her past experience to fund the groceries.

Now if this second wife bails out of the arrangement, the husband should not despair. Having lived with two wives, he should now understand more about himself and his needs. For the third wife, he should be able to choose a woman who will complement him best. He will through natural affection want to spend time with her. And by this time, he will probably also have received a raise. That extra income will allow him to share some with his wife for her use. This attention should appease the third wife and give her the sense of fulfillment she seeks so that the two can live out their years in a fruitful partnership.

What! Am I crazy to suggest such a thing? Of course. The above scenario is absurd. But it's the very scenario churches and pastors are currently playing out when hiring associates. Lyle Schaller, in *Survival Tactics in the Parish,* even suggests not becoming the first assistant to fill a position, but the third—or at least to follow someone who's enjoyed a pleasant tenure.[1] As Esa summarizes the reason:

> The first associate a church hires is often a
> young, inexperienced minister just out of seminary.
> Little thought has been given as to how the new
> position will function within the church's overall
> ministry. Consequently, the young minister—often
> feeling excluded, ignored, and overlooked—resigns
> after a short stint. Blaming the failed relationship on
> the immaturity of the young minister, the church

often will seek another associate with more experience. However, little is done to change the church's structure to accommodate two pastors in its ministry. Again after a short tenure, the second associate pastor finds a new call. By the third attempt, the church has finally learned how to accept and productively use two pastors in its leadership.[2]

Before creating a new associate position, thought and planning needs to go into the position's function and relationship to the church. The assistant role should be a position with purposeful intent to carry out a specific part of God's plan. This should not be a cop-out, overflow position.

Donald Sevetson asserts that an associate pastor usually comes on staff because "senior ministers seek someone to whom they can turn over those parts of their workload which they feel they can safely leave to someone else."[3] Associates, on the other hand, seek the position mainly because the salary is better than a tiny church pastorate, because he doesn't want the demands and structure of the senior ministry, and because he feels he will escape the fishbowl life for his family.

These reasons, although part of the overall equation, should rank below issues of calling and design. When they don't, "the 'team,' then, often consists of two men who have no intention of subordinating their individual needs or vocational goals to any overall style. Both are trying to find a convenient, acceptable way to 'do their thing.' Each intends to have the other do the part of the ministerial task that he likes the least, and it doesn't take long to spot the trouble ahead in a relationship in which each party is concerned primarily about what he gets out of it for himself."[4]

What are we as the body of Christ doing? We need a new model. Before a senior pastor or church leadership creates a new associate role or fills a vacant one, they must first recognize that role as equal in importance and priority to the senior pastor's. It cannot be a cast-off position. It cannot be a position just to fill in the gaps.

In days past, when a log cabin had gaps in its structure, the owner filled the holes with wood chinks. If drafts blew inside, the owner patched or plugged it up. That's how we currently tend to hire assistants—as plugs.

Senior pastors and administrative leadership, let's not hire assistant pastors as chinks and patches. Let's plan and build whole, new, architecturally sound walls. Create positions that can make use of someone's design and call—within the vision of your church—to better serve the members.

Deciding to hire an assistant means letting go of some control over certain areas. Great! You'll have more time for preaching, praying, and teaching—or whatever it is that the leadership decides is right for you to do.

In "Giants Growing Giants," Dennis Fields writes, "Many pastors feel that in certain areas no one can achieve the desired response as effectively as they can. This is not a negative character quality. It is a positive leadership trait. Pastors who are honest with themselves recognize their own leadership deficiencies. These deficiencies should be the strengths of the associate."[5] Absolutely. Your ministry doesn't have to look like another senior pastor's. Align your job to your strengths and find an associate whose strengths and passion are your deficiencies.

For that matter, in many senior/associate relationships, "both men have strengths which are probably being ignored because of their job descriptions. They should be ready and willing to make the switches that experience dictates regardless of the congregation's expectations."[6] When the senior pastor and leadership start looking at the associate as a co-laborer in Christ rather than an underling, the shifts in expected roles can take place for the benefit of everyone.

Choosing the Right Associate

Once the leadership knows its own strengths and weaknesses, once you have created a specific plan for including the new minister as a respected player on the team—and written the job description—where do you start looking for the right assistant? Schaller warns against immediately jumping to the familiar:

> History is filled with stories of pastors who invited an old acquaintance or a longtime friend to come and serve as the new associate. It was assumed that since they were personally compatible, they would be professionally compatible.

Sometimes they were. All too often they found themselves personally compatible at first, but that was soon erased by the fact that they were not professionally compatible; and they separated with strained or broken friendships. The minister who is looking at a stranger as his or her potential associate is more likely to examine the potential professional compatibility much more carefully than the minister who is discussing this proposed relationship with a friend.[7]

Make sure you have your potential candidates fill out personality tests and gift assessments. Remember, you are looking for a person to round out your ministry, not to mimic it. Share your own strengths and weaknesses honestly. You're not necessarily looking for opposites but complementary traits—and you need to have a clear idea of what the ideal assistant looks like to you. Include personalities, skills, and spiritual gifts in the mix.

Do you need a technician? A teacher? Or a people-person and public relations man? What is your work style, and how would someone need to fit into that format?

Determine what category of assistant might work best for your church. What are your long-term goals? An *intentional* assistant can bring stability. An *unintentional* assistant can fill in more temporarily, but will also bring strong senior pastor-type gifts to the mix. Think about how you can use those gifts to benefit the church. An unintentional *pastor,* returning to the associate ministry will bring experience, but he will also need encouragement and a soft place to land. Can you offer that?

Ask about how the candidate sees himself in the next five or ten years. (This assesses among other things his view of middle-range planning.) Be up front about the financial package, what it does and doesn't offer. And of course, pray, pray, pray for the people and the process.

Caring for the Associate Pastor

Whether the body is congregationally led, elder led, or has the multilayered hierarchal stratum of some denominations, the senior pastor sets the tone at the local level. His priorities become the church's priorities. His viewpoints become the congregation's. If the senior pastor is ministering well, his influence drives the local church. In order for there to be any change in how associate pastors are perceived and received, the senior pastor must be aware that the calling of the assistant pastor is equal to his own calling. He must not only be aware of the worth of the associate's call; he must respect it. He must honor the assistant as the members naturally honor his own role, and he must lead the congregation in adopting that same viewpoint.

The care for the associate starts even before you find the right man by making sure that you are creating or filling a position that can satisfy the desires of a man who wants to minister effectively for the Lord. When you find that man whom

God has called to your church to serve alongside you, be sure to welcome him, set him up for success, and educate the congregation on the appropriate way to treat this man of God.

Welcome Him In

So now you've hired an assistant. By all means let the congregation get to know him and his family—especially that part of the body he will specialize over, if applicable. Have welcome committees that come from the area he will supervise. Let the adult Sunday school teachers get to know the Christian education pastor. Arrange for your vocal, instrumental, dramatic, and artistic talent to meet and greet the new worship director. Encourage the crowd with evangelistic gifts to knock on the new outreach pastor's door and help him move in—unannounced, of course.

At the same time, make sure that those assistants who too often become pigeonholed—the youth pastor, the administrative pastor, and the mission pastor, for example—have ample time to be seen and greeted by the entire congregation. A five-minute introduction in one service is not enough. Make him visible over time until people know who he is and what he does.

The senior pastor and his family should also take special time to express a personal interest in the well-being of the new associate and his family. This initial interaction will communicate loudly how the leadership perceives the new staff person—as a threat to the status quo, as a wheelbarrow in which to dump all the extra pressures and disliked tasks, or as a respected member of the ministry team. Be aware, however, that while "the senior pastor may hope to have a family-like relationship with staff members, being an effective boss, as well as an amiable co-laborer, is easier said than done. A sensitive and caring associate pastor may know of the heart concerns and needs of other staff members and parishioners before a senior pastor discovers these matters."[8]

That's OK. But it doesn't give the senior pastor an excuse to avoid the issue. Sevetson tells senior pastors, "Most of you subconsciously see your associates as threats instead of helps. Acknowledge it. From such honesty real strength can grow."[9] Make sure your attitude and your attention are welcoming. Invite him in, get to know him, and find out how his strengths can benefit the body.

Part of welcoming the new assistant will be to acclimate him to the inner workings of the staff. As I discussed in the last chapter, the church leadership or senior pastor and the associate must have a clear understanding of what each expects from the arrangement and how this expectation will be fulfilled. But not everything needed can or will be written in the job description. "Once the senior pastor decides to hire an associate, he should begin a period of 'indoctrination,' when he explains his vision, his methods, his priorities, his goals, and his view of himself as a leader. The senior pastor should explain the areas where he expects the associate to become strongly involved and those areas where he should remain passive."[10]

This explanation should not come as a surprise to the associate. It should have been discussed in the interview process and only reiterated later, but it is worth going over again.

Set Up for Success

In the welcoming in of the new associate, make sure you're setting him up for success and not failure. When introducing a new assistant, the hiring committee must be careful to explain the reasons for the assistant's hire and the realistic scope of work he will be expected to perform: "Usually the church leadership 'sell' the second minister to the congregation on the basis of increased services and convenience. Everything from the generation gap to the problem of keeping up with the other prestige churches in town is dragged in as justification for adding 'staff.'"[11] Don't get caught up in "selling" the new associate.

If the current pastor(s) are overwhelmed by their growing church, don't avoid saying you need help just to keep up with what you could previously accomplish by yourselves. Admitting you can't do it all is not weak; it's good leadership. Praise the church for its growth!

If the assistant will be taking over an established program or building a new one, explain the vision but without creating a superhuman assistant in the process. Overemphasizing a new assistant's abilities and benefits will only cause the congregation dissatisfaction when the assistant fails to perform.

Sometimes senior pastors build up assistants too much. The pastor says, "I'm bringing in a man who's specially gifted in this area. He's really going to put our youth program together for us." He's building the image of this new staff person by explaining what he hopes *might* be accomplished. The congregation will be saying, "Great! We've got a miracle worker coming." Then they find out he's not who they expected. They expected somebody who could walk on water, and this guy only walks on land!

Realize that by pumping him up to the church, trying to sell him and to sell the position, you're going to hurt the staff member and all that he might bring with him. He may not fill all the dreams that you had; he may widen your vision to new dreams. He's an individual designed by God with gifts, traits, and ideas peculiar to him. Allow him the latitude and the respect to create within the boundaries of his job description, using his skills and his passion. Rather than oversell, explain to the congregation the true need. And then allow them opportunities to see what the assistant is accomplishing. By seeing his good efforts, they will gain confidence in him.

Educate and Engage the Congregation

James Berkley, an associate editor of *Leadership* magazine, developed a survey to discover the qualities that the assistant liked most about his senior pastor's supervision. He came up with four qualities:

1. Latitude
2. Individuality

3. Recognition
4. Support[12]

Latitude can be defined as giving a subordinate significant responsibility and trust in carrying out responsibilities. In individuality, associates appreciated personal attention. Similarly, in recognition, associates appreciated that recognition was even given to their contributions. Support was valued mostly by younger assistants; however, all voiced the need for emotional and physical support.

The senior pastor needs to support his staff, but he can't do it alone. Let the congregation help. Teach them how. The congregation is usually unaware of the intricate working of the assistant and associate pastors. In my new paradigm, it is not an option but a must that the congregation be involved in the associates' lives. Often hired by the senior pastor, assistants are seen as a part of his staff. Subsequently, the congregation feels they have only an indirect responsibility to be involved. The changes that need to occur in this area happen only at the senior pastor's urging and instruction.

Support Teams. Because pastors are seen as ministering to others, few people are aware of the drain and strain this causes. Members of the congregation frequently minister to the senior pastor, but assistants are often forgotten. Many assistants are emotionally bankrupt because of the lack of consideration and concern from others.

Here are some recommendations to help your church address this problem. The congregation can form support teams around each of the assistants as is often done for the senior pastor. Divide the teams into several family groups that are assigned to minister to the assistant and his family. People should be paying attention to every aspect of the assistant's needs.

Prayer. The teams should include members who specifically pray with and for the associates—not only during times of emotional crisis but also as a regular routine. These prayer requests can be as specific as the assistant will allow and must be taken before our Savior on a daily and as-needed basis.

Tangible Assistance. During high emotional trauma or illness of the associate or his family, members should assist in any way possible to make the burden bearable. Most churches are good at this, but my experience tells me that many an assistant and even a senior pastor are left with the hollow statement, "Call me if you need me," which means nothing. The new paradigm of the congregation's response to an assistant calls for seeing things that can be done and then doing them. It can be as simple as making calls on his behalf.

Preparing meals, cutting the lawn, cleaning the house, picking up laundry, and many other tangible expressions like these can lift a person's burdens. Requests must be done as ministry, not expecting any reward. Ministry during emotionally stressed times is rarely forgotten by those who've been ministered to. Bearing one another's burdens and loving one another are only a few of the many deeds that can aid in the process of ministering to the assistant.

Financial Concern. Likewise, congregations must be aware of the financial needs of the staff member's family. Though this is a highly personal area, some members must get close enough to establish when there may be legitimate financial needs. Finances are only discussed with the intimate few who have paid the price of a relationship that goes beyond the surface of smooth talk. All members aren't able to share at this level. Yet, when allowed, some people must know how to help in this area.

Struggling financially can be the reason why assistants, who are often underpaid, consider second jobs and major changes of ministry. Sometimes the appeal may be salary related, budget related, or a short-term need. Methods of remedying the situation must be prayed about, reviewed, and a plan of action established with short-range and long-range effects. Assistants and their families have just as much need for stabilized financial compensation as everyone else. They work hard, and the laborer is worthy of his wages.

Community Needs. As in the areas of emotional and financial needs, so must the congregation be interested in the assistant's social and educational needs. The families of assistants, as others, have a need to be wanted, cared for, and related with their families. Their children need to identify with other children and be able to form social bonds critical to the happy transitioning of the entire family. Invite them over for dinner or to social functions outside the church. Many now in our congregation have access to sporting event tickets and can use them as a wonderful tool for social bonding among families.

The Role of Mentoring

Perhaps the greatest contribution a senior pastor can make to the assistant position is to consistently disciple and mentor. He should mentor not only the intern who wants to learn how to become a senior pastor, or the intentional associate and unintentional pastor who will need to understand and tangibly fulfill his vision, but also the leadership in the church and the young men and women who will rise up to become disciple makers themselves one day. One of the greatest ways to find an associate who will fit in your church is to spend time mentoring and getting to know the young people with a heart for ministry.

As Paul stated to young Timothy, "And the things which you have heard from me in the presence of many witnesses, these entrust to faithful men, who will be able to teach others also" (2 Tim. 2:2). Good ministry—good leadership—involves multiplying one's effectiveness through raising up new leaders to proclaim the gospel. The time that it takes to invest in the spiritual growth and training of others will be returned as they become able to carry some of the burden themselves.

Dennis Fields writes, "Training an associate is a learning experience for the senior pastor as well. He strengthens his communication skills as he teaches by word and example. The pastor may have forgotten some of the traits that served to make him successful, but as he imparts his knowledge and experience to the associate, he may rekindle fires of zeal.

'Iron sharpeneth iron; so a man sharpeneth the countenance of his friend'" (Prov. 27:17).[13]

Senior pastors must make time to disciple their assistants. Some of the proof of Moses' mentoring skills can be seen in Joshua's success as he transitioned from assistant to leader. Evidently, in the first chapter of Joshua, Joshua was scared. God told him at least three times in chapter 1 to be strong and of good courage, indicating that Joshua was weak or faint of heart and God needed to encourage him. Perhaps Joshua didn't feel up to the task. (Remember Moses' earlier fear and protestations in this same situation?) We can imagine Joshua thinking, *I don't want to follow this man. He was a great leader. How can I measure up?*

But Joshua had learned from his mentor. He didn't question God's appointment. And God responded favorably by bolstering him with words indicating that *He* would be in charge and would always be with Joshua.

Because Joshua recognized the magnitude of his responsibility toward God and his people, he came into this job with total dependence on God. He had no choice. And that's what made him a great leader. He learned from Moses the necessity of depending on God, first as an assistant, yet even more so as the person in charge.

The other characteristic that shows both Moses' mentoring skills and Joshua's own leadership skills is Joshua's understanding of his own design. Although he watched Moses, although he did everything that Moses showed him to do, he never tried to become Moses. And therefore, Joshua became just what God made him. He was the warrior, the military man, when the Israelites needed a warrior. Where Moses had been a theologian of sorts, Joshua was strictly a military man. We don't see him coming up with much strong theology of any sort except at the end of his tenure when he told the people to make a choice. But "as for me and my house, we will serve the LORD" (Josh. 24:15).

Although Joshua learned from Moses, they were different leaders. Joshua was quiet and reserved. He didn't seem to get mad at the people for anything or get angry. He just took them through a military campaign. He was the leader whom God wanted for that particular time in Israel's history.

The Art of Mentoring

The book of Acts gives us a detailed view of how Barnabas and Paul related in the ministry. Because of Paul's great legacy through Scripture, Barnabas is often dismissed as a minor character in comparison. But, as I mentioned previously, he was an important person who mentored Paul and knew when to step aside to allow God's plan to take effect.

Special note should be given to the name Barnabas. Known as "the Son of Encouragement," Barnabas was used by God to befriend Paul, who was looked upon with skepticism by other believers. Paul needed the touch of a leader who could mentor or uphold him after his conversion. Barnabas, the consummate encourager, provided that touch.

For all practical purposes Barnabas became Saul's

mentor. Howard and William Hendricks describe special qualities one must have to be a mentor:

(1) He promotes genuine growth and change. The goal of every mentor should be the emotional, social, and spiritual growth of his protégé or the person he mentors.

(2) A mentor provides a model to follow.

(3) A mentor helps you to reach your goals more efficiently.

(4) A mentor plays a key role in God's pattern for your growth.

(5) A mentor's influence benefits others in your life.[14]

Barnabas fulfilled every one of these characteristics as he groomed Paul for the ministry.

When Paul left Damascus for Jerusalem after his conversion, he struggled to reach the disciples. Barnabas did not stand idly by observing, but he found out about Paul, "took hold of him and brought him to the apostles" (Acts 9:27). Barnabas stepped in and mediated the relationship between Paul and the apostles, moving it along to a relationship of trust sooner than Paul could have done by himself. Certainly Paul had a strength that defied all resistance to his preaching the gospel of Christ, but can you imagine how Barnabas's actions and belief in his sincerity bolstered Paul's spirit and resolve?

Barnabas seems to have always kept his eyes open for a ministry slot that would fit God's calling on Paul's life. After Barnabas had ministered in Antioch and discovered the environment, he didn't stay and pine for a helper, and he didn't pray for God to give Paul a similar ministry; instead, he left his post and sought out Paul in Tarsus (Acts 11:25). Barnabas had a special insight into Paul's strengths, and he helped him to define and refine his gift of teaching by developing those who were in Antioch.

The Holy Spirit validated Barnabas's insight into Paul's calling by commissioning Barnabas and Paul to go on the first missionary journey (Acts 13:1–2). During that trip, the leadership transfer occurred. The text begins to refer to Paul as Paul instead of Saul, and it is after Paul's mighty sermon at Paphos that the text begins to refer to the pair as "Paul and Barnabas" rather than "Barnabas and Paul." Paul gained top billing. He came into his own senior pastorate role.

Mentoring with Intimacy

Paul learned the importance of mentoring with a personal touch. Soon after splitting from Barnabas, Paul chose to guide young Timothy (Acts 16:1–3).

Throughout his ministry Paul discipled several assistant leaders, yet Scripture shows us in detail the personal touch of his communication with Timothy. In Acts 16:1–3, Paul is introduced to Timothy, who had a unique set of circumstances. Timothy's mother was Jewish, but his father was Greek. Since Timothy was so well spoken of by the people in the area, Paul insisted that he be circumcised. Paul was intuitive to the Spirit's leading by seeing in Timothy that he would be used in the gospel ministry. This relationship became more evident as he wrote to Timothy in his epistles known as the Pastoral Epistles.

Paul spoke as a father in 1 Timothy 1:2: "To Timothy, my true child in the faith: Grace, mercy and peace from God the Father and Christ Jesus our Lord." The term of endearment used here implies that Paul was responsible for mentoring Timothy in his spiritual growth and development. Verse 18 follows with Paul mentoring Timothy and using the term "my son," which indicated the spiritual leadership role Paul assumed in Timothy's life. As a father who expected refinement in his son, Paul knew Timothy, a spiritual baby, required this nurturing. Later in the same book, Paul is clear about his intent and lets Timothy know of his desire to be with him.

It is imperative for the future growth of the kingdom of God that senior pastors have a fond affection for young assistants in their congregations. A spiritual model must be seen long before it can be heard. Paul's model of fatherly affection allowed him to grow Timothy in every area of his personality and character.

In 2 Timothy, Paul's intimacy increased. He was in prison, and his words were weighted with a sense of urgency. Paul greeted Timothy as "my beloved son: Grace, mercy and peace from God the Father and Christ Jesus our Lord" (2 Tim. 1:2). In the second chapter he continued, "You therefore, my son, be strong in the grace that is in Christ Jesus" (2 Tim. 2:1). Paul also reaffirmed Timothy by stating, "I am mindful of the sincere faith within you, which first dwelt in your grandmother Lois, and your mother Eunice, and I am sure that it is in you as well" (2 Tim. 1:5).

Senior pastors would do well to be specific yet personal in their affirmation of their assistants. Too often we hear horror stories about the division among staff ministers because of lack of proper personal attention. Paul's lessons of encouragement, discipleship, fathering, mentoring, teaching, and admonishing is a dynamic model for senior pastors and assistant pastors to study.

I thank God for a relationship with Dr. Evans, my senior pastor, that allowed for my growth in literally every area of my life. Though I am chronologically older, Dr. Evans's model of leadership inspires me to greater heights in Christ. This can be achieved only through an openness, at times, to be vulnerable with each other. Senior pastors need not stop to talk about it, but let the modeling emerge through daily events. Hospital visits, weddings, communion, funerals, speaking engagements, counseling couples, encouraging singles, Bible study preparation, and many other events provide natural times to mentor assistants. Though laborious, these times are laboratories and are also God's cameos of what the assistant can do to lighten the load of the senior pastor. Pastors can seize these moments as God-structured times to train and mentor.

Mentoring with Humility

The senior pastor should mentor even the intern who is after his job. Even if a young assistant or a young intern bad-mouths you or says things about you that are not true, you still have the responsibility of making that person effective.

Look at Peter. The fallen one among Jesus' disciples, Peter took the leadership of the church after the crisis. Even in death, Christ was discipling. And Peter began to espouse God's plan. Do you see who Christ left at the head? The one who always had his foot in his mouth. He left the one who always appeared to be in the center of controversy. But Jesus recognized Peter's potential and guided him to it.

Barnabas understood this concept. Following his heated discussion with Paul about John Mark's dedication, Barnabas chose to leave Paul and take John Mark under his wing. Barnabas's mentoring duties to Paul had been fulfilled. Now John Mark needed his special touch. Barnabas's willingness to risk his reputation on the development of a young minister provided for John Mark the needed affirmation to ignite him into the responsibility of the gospel ministry. Once again, Barnabas fulfilled his name—Encourager.

Senior pastors must be able to see what God sees in developing the assistant. There are times when this is the only transmitter God uses to aid in the development of others. Barnabas's approach to ministry was rare, yet needed. Vision for God's kingdom must always include the discipling of those closest to you.

A Bountiful Journey

Assistant pastors are often forgotten as God's people who need special attention. As a senior pastor, you are mentoring and discipling your congregation. You are ministering to your congregation's needs and arranging for help to be available. Consider whether you are also exhibiting these qualities in how you relate to your staff.

A respondent to a survey about assistant pastors a few years ago wrote:

> I believe I am just about in the best case scenario. The relationship and affinity of purpose-driven direction between the senior pastor and myself are paramount to creating this environment we enjoy. We are a perfect match. Second, the congregation's high view of pastoral leadership has helped the environment. Third, when pastors who are competent leaders, who model biblical servant/ God direct ministry that is backed up by people accepting Christ and discipling people to become fully devoted followers of Christ, Satan will have problems getting a foothold.[15]

The senior pastor should be an example of serving others, realizing that Philippians 2:3–5 requires him to see the quality of the associate's position before God. Within the local body, most recognize that the senior pastor is often the higher person of authority. But from God's viewpoint the persons are equal, with differing gifts and responsibilities expressed through serving one another and the congregation. Senior pastors who fail to see assistants as gifted servants will often tilt the vision of the congregation to misunderstand the pastoral support staff. On the other hand, openness about their respective callings can begin the journey of a fruitful relationship.

Chapter Six

Why We Rehearse: Learning How to Work Together

Then they said, "Let us arise and build." So they put their
hands to the good work. (Neh. 2:18b)

Take small children outside, and they will delight in naming everything they see and hear. You will expect their sweet voices to say the word *birdie* or some such approximation. Why is this true? When we tune out all the traffic and city noise, we notice that bird chatter remains constant. It doesn't matter if the birds are saying, "Hey, where are you?" or "Watch out for that cat!" The fact remains that they continue a volley of communication all day long. When the birds are *not* talking, that's when we know something's wrong. It's such a common premise that moviemakers often use their silence as a signal. *What's going to happen?* you think. *It's too quiet.*

Communication in the ministry should be constant *and* real. As Jesus' ministry grew, He "would often slip away to the wilderness and pray" (Luke 5:16). Despite—and in fact because of—the union he shared with the Father and the Spirit, he took time with God to foster their relationship, to share needs, and to ask for help. He didn't wait until a problem arose to sit down and talk; he made it a regular habit.

"We talk," you say. OK. But about what? And how do you talk? Are you truly connecting with everyone in your park? Or are you just making noise?

True Connection

For associates and senior pastors to minister well together, they must relate well to one another. David and Jonathan had a unique relationship. The eldest son of King Saul, Jonathan probably would have inherited the throne. He was expected to honor his father the king above all else. Yet after David killed Goliath, Scripture states that "the soul of Jonathan was knit to the soul of David, and Jonathan loved him as himself" (1 Sam. 18:1).

In human terms, Jonathan should have protected his own position as crown prince and his father's reputation. Instead, Jonathan befriended the man whom others used to taunt Saul: "Saul has slain his thousands, and David his ten thousands" (1 Sam. 18:7). More than once he defended

David against Saul (1 Sam. 19:1–7; 20:32, 38, 42). Why? Perhaps Jonathan had a natural affinity for the young man who lived with his family. But I think the better answer is that Jonathan loved David because he appreciated his character, his action, and his drive to glorify God. Saul was losing the kingdom by his ungodly actions; David was gaining it with his godly deeds.

Even if your ministry team doesn't always agree on issues, even if you have difficulty connecting with a member of the staff, do you appreciate each person's drive to glorify God, to create his kingdom here on earth, and to be the person God delights for him to be? Even if, other than being on staff together, you might have never picked this person to call a friend, can you see reasons that God has put him in this place? That's where true comradeship begins— not just in the easy friendship with those most like you, but in those relationships where the bond of godly brotherhood can overcome the differences.

As I said earlier, the personalities of the senior pastor and the associate will probably—and probably should— differ. These differences, without good communication, can lead to misunderstandings and conflict. To minister effectively as a team, you must be able to appreciate your teammates. And in order to appreciate them, you need to know who they are. You must communicate. You must *learn* to communicate—no matter how many classes you've taken on the subject, although they are helpful. You must learn to communicate with *these* people, *this* pastor. You must practice communication from true connection rather than from assumption. You must take the idea of communication and slide it clear across the bar to comradeship.

What You Thought You Knew

As Dr. Evans and I began to work together, I expected to have to learn about the relationship. But before long, I thought I had grasped how things should go. When one of our members fell into sin, I assumed that our response should be instant discipline. Dr. Evans disagreed. He felt that before we could act, we had to develop a whole discipline process. Very quickly I discovered that I would need to come up with an idea for a thoroughly working relationship. I needed to learn how to keep up with Dr. Evans's ideas and thinking.

Another time, we were discussing Wednesday night utilization at our church. My Baptist church background meant that I saw Wednesday nights as prayer meeting nights and nothing else. Dr. Evans, on the other hand, envisioned a new style for us. Communicating on this point meant that he had to patiently reiterate the whole philosophy at Oak Cliff, and I had to be willing to change my thinking—to reevaluate whether my preconceived notions were tied directly to theology, or whether I could stretch my ideas to include the senior pastor's vision. He needed to unveil his vision and philosophy to me; I needed to listen well and bring myself in line with his leadership style.

Communication isn't just about discussing—or arguing—the issues. It's about taking the time to bring up what others need to know, and listening very carefully with intent to understand what the other person is expecting. It is so easy to fall into assumption and not really hear what the other person is saying. Or worse yet, you might assume that everybody knows what you're thinking, although you haven't told them.

Every Issue Is Important

After David fled from Saul's wrath, he sought an answer from Jonathan. At first Jonathan did not believe David's accusation against Saul could be true. He said, "Behold, my father does nothing either great or small without disclosing it to me. So why should my father hide this thing from me? It is not so!" (1 Sam. 20:2). But even in his grief and disbelief, Jonathan did not dismiss David's question or ignore it. When David explained, Jonathan understood that David would not ask lightly. He answered, "Whatever you say, I will do for you" (1 Sam. 20:4). And then Jonathan followed through. Even when he discovered that his own throne would never be established if David lived, Jonathan chose to protect God's chosen one over his own position (1 Sam. 20:31).

Of course, David's life or death was an important issue, but we don't always realize the gravity of an issue until we have heard it and searched it out. Communication means that if one of the two people thinks an issue is important, it *is* important. When the pastor says he needs to talk to you about something, you should respond, "Set a time; I'm ready." At the same time, the pastor should give you equal respect and an equal audience.

To develop such respect, the associate must learn discrimination with what he brings to the pastor so that he's not crying wolf every five days. The senior pastor is a busy man. He doesn't need to hear about every little incident that's going on in the church. Usually there's a lot of minor matters going on that he doesn't need to hear about. When he says that it's something he wants to know, be sure you keep him informed and tell him everything. Other than that, the assistant needs to determine which issues the senior pastor needs to handle and what should be managed as his responsibility. Then when he says to the senior pastor, "Listen, this is an important issue," the pastor will be willing to listen because he knows the associate doesn't interrupt his day for minor "stuff."

Our system called for having a regularly scheduled time once or twice a month when we talked about the serious issues of the church and where things were going. For instance, we talked about things I needed to have prepared for the elders meeting, things I needed to have prepared for some ministry team, or things that I needed to oversee in the church. We took time to talk. And whenever there had been a discussion where Dr. Evans had given me a task that I felt was outside my job description, I said, "I will try my best to get it done." And he expected me to do it.

Now I'm not as timely as I'd like to be, but he knew I'd get it done. And I got it done to the best interest of the church and everyone involved. The important thing is not only that you follow through, but that you do the job so well that you know the church will be proud of the way you did it, and the senior pastor will know he can trust what you say. The issue is important to him; it should be important to you.

Openness and Honesty

True communication—communication that moves to comradeship—must be open and honest. Despite our Lord's saving work that has freed us from enslavement to sin, we are a broken people. Many have spoken of the church as a hospital. Especially because of this fact, you must invite openness among the staff, or at the very least between the associates and the senior pastor. Starting from the first contact, prospective assistants should be frank about their expectations and needs as well as invite the same courtesy from the senior pastor and hiring committee. Then as the job becomes reality, you must work to maintain open and honest communication.

On a certain occasion, a staff member, who was being used improperly, became unhappy with me. But instead of coming to me with the problem, this person went over my head to complain to Dr. Evans. That hurt me. In all honesty, it made me angry. As fellow workers in Christ, we need to treat one another as brothers. We need to be approachable, not defensive, and we need to address concerns directly with the perceived offender, not with supervisors and not as gossip to others. We need communication that creates a connection.

The same thing happens with Dr. Evans. There are a lot of people who would use me to get to him. And I know they use me to get to him. I just tell them that they may need to talk directly with him. Such events inevitably happen, whether the complainer is a staff member, a volunteer, or someone from the congregation. But whether the complaint is against me or shared with me against Dr. Evans, he and I have talked it through and decided that we would not honor the complaint unless that person had first discussed it with the offending party.

By open and honest, I'm not saying be brutally blunt. At times we have to say the hard things, but as Paul writes, "Let no unwholesome word proceed from your mouth, but only such a word as is good for edification according to the need of the moment, so that it will give grace to those who hear" (Eph. 4:29). Always think of building up the pastor. Not only is this commanded by Scripture; it is the assistant's specific job to do so. Even when you need to discuss a negative situation, turn it into a positive statement and build him up as a person.

Quiet in the Park

Not everyone needs the same amount of conversation to find a connection. Some pastors are quiet and easygoing, and you have to press them to keep the communication lines open. Although this can be frustrating, I would advise assistants in this situation to say what they want to say, and then leave the senior pastor alone. Don't drag him through a long conversation about a problem. Say what you need to say, give him a chance to respond, and go. If you need his answer or direction, tell him so. Chances are, he'll speak up when it's important. As long as he moves in when he's really needed, he is expressing confidence in your ability with his silence. When working alongside this type of personality, you might have to initiate conversations when you feel he should have done so. Pay more attention to his response to your initiative than his ability to initiate himself.

Some assistants might say, "My pastor never responds to me." That speaks volumes as well. If he never gets to your issues because he "forgot," then you need to ask other questions. Maybe it's time to evaluate what you want and what you are accomplishing in this situation. It's time to say, "It's too quiet . . . what's about to happen here?"

Next to Him

Communication and comradeship. With all of our human failings, these are tall orders but necessary. To model God's kingdom on earth, those who minister to the body must be able to lead in unity—to work alongside one another, not despite one another.

In the book of Nehemiah, the Jewish remnant rose up with Nehemiah to carry out God's will in rebuilding the wall around Jerusalem. They worked together, each building his own portion of the wall so that the task could be accomplished in full. When they experienced opposition from Sanballat, they worked out a system to summon each other with a trumpet so that they could protect themselves as well as continue their work. And by working together with one purpose, by helping each other with basic needs, and by repenting from practicing usury on their brothers, they got the wall rebuilt.

In our new understanding of the associate ministry, the pastoral staff needs to learn to work in a similar way. As Nehemiah 3 points out, none of the believing remnant put on airs or claimed he was above the work that needed to be done. Instead, each person worked "next to him," and he in turn worked "next to him" who also worked "next to him," and so on. With everyone's work respected and expected, the people were able to restore the wall.

Not only do we need to work "next" to each other, but we also need to communicate affirmation to those with whom we work. Consider how Paul treated his many ministry assistants. Romans 16 contains sixteen verses of greetings and recognition of those who had worked alongside him. In 2 Corinthians 8:23, Paul spoke of Titus as his "partner and fellow worker." He called Epaphroditus his "brother and fellow worker and fellow soldier," also thanking God for Epaphroditus's recovery "lest I should have sorrow upon sorrow" (Phil. 2:25, 27). He called Timothy his "brother and God's fellow worker in the gospel of

Christ" (1 Thess. 3:2). And he greeted Philemon as his "beloved brother and fellow worker," thanking God for him "because I hear of your love, and of the faith which you have toward the Lord Jesus, and toward all the saints; and I pray that the fellowship of your faith may become effective through the knowledge of every good thing which is in you for Christ's sake" (Philem. 1, 5–6).

These fellow workers weren't perfect, but Paul focused on their love for Christ; he recognized the care and labor he had received from them, and he made them his comrades for the sake of the gospel. But most importantly, he communicated his love and concern to them.

Needed Professionally

Sometimes you just get bogged down with your everyday responsibilities. I'm trying to get my job done, and he's trying to get his job done—and sometimes the environment gets almost competitive instead of encouraging. I tried to train myself over the years to go back and give encouragement. When you see a good job, recognize it. Identify that person, and say "well done." That compliment may be the only one the staff member has heard in awhile.

Right now, my staff and I are planning special luncheons for all the pastors here, and not just as a group. We'll meet with each of them individually so we can talk to him and say, "We appreciate your work, we appreciate you, and my office appreciates you." They will get to eat a nice lunch off of us, but more importantly we will have taken the time to connect with them, to ward off the ministry burnout so often caused by lack of appreciation and neglect.

Needed Personally

As much as they need professional encouragement, assistants and pastors alike need personal encouragement and spiritual care even more. Those teams that work well together take the time to provide this ministry for one another.

For a long time, I considered myself the master of care and caring for the people in the church. I thought that if people raised their heads and said they needed caring, I would be there. I loved that job, and I felt it was a part of my giftedness to be a servant—an aide—especially in times of difficulty.

One day we got a letter from one of our members. Paraphrased, it said, "When you get this letter, I'll be dead because nobody cared for me." And though she had sent it to the church and to Dr. Evans as well as myself, I felt that I had let her down. I had let the church down. I had let myself down. I had let everything down. I was emotionally devastated. I cried out in my heart, "Oh God, I cost this girl her life!" I took it personally—very personally.

Then I remember Dr. Evans encouraging me and saying, "Listen Hawk, we can't stop things like this." When I felt like God was not pleased with my work, when I felt that I had failed, Dr. Evans reached out to make sure I was OK. He probably felt horrible himself at the time, but I was drowning. I felt like God was smashing me in the face with a woman who had committed suicide.

I remember some of the members calling me, too, saying, "You've done as well with caring as anybody in the church can, and you just can't get to everybody." Those few little words of encouragement picked me up. They meant everything to me. Without this encouragement, I could have been permanently scarred into believing that I just didn't have what it took. But with that encouragement, I increased the intensity of the care cells that we had operating at the church. And it worked out that we did begin to care much more specifically for the people.

The need for care goes both ways. Senior pastors, while they may hold their own counsel because of their leadership position, need just as much encouragement as the next staff person. Just because he gives his spiritual wisdom to the church doesn't mean he is ready to handle whatever life throws him. I can remember going in to talk to Dr. Evans during a rough period when his parents, who were getting older, kept getting sicker. It was a point of concern, and it was pulling him down while he was trying to do his job.

Another time, he had to have a minor operation. And even though he had told us not to come to the hospital, I went and prayed with him that morning anyhow. I said something to make him laugh. I told him that I came just so I could see him in that gown with the back end out so I could report it to the congregation. He fell out on the sheets laughing. "Hawk, no one would do nothing crazy like that but you," he told me.

"You got that right!" I replied. "I planned to come with a camera to take a picture of you in this situation, but I couldn't find the camera. So I'll just have to tell everybody that you looked just like all of us in this gown!"

A Work in Progress

Learning to work with a group of people takes time. And it can't happen without open and honest communication. Turning work and ministry relationships into comradeships may be one of the hardest jobs you will encounter in the ministry. But if God has put you on a team, he wants you to love and appreciate your teammates so you can model his character to your flock. To do so, some of your most open and honest communication must be with the Lord. Pray for your fellow workers. Look and ask for ways to affirm them and their ministries, and always thank God for them. When the senior pastor and the associates find this unity, the label of the chair each sits in will not matter.

Chapter Seven

Discord:
When the Orchestra Is out of Tune

Behold, how good and how pleasant it is
For brothers to dwell together in unity!
(Ps. 133:1)

Sometimes, no matter what you do, you will find your orchestra out of tune. You've picked great staff members. You've tried to spread out the gifts and traits among the positions rather than hire identical personalities. You've built in time for communication and mentoring. But the song still doesn't sound right.

Remember back in the beginning when we talked about the concertmaster entering the stage and giving the note to which everyone must tune his or her instrument? Before the concertmaster came on stage, he had to tune and check his violin against a standardized tone, something that wouldn't fluctuate with the humidity or stretch with age. Often, church staff members try to do the same thing as the concertmaster. They've had training. They can interpret the Bible as well as the senior pastor. Why doesn't their tuning themselves to these "standardized" sources allow them to enter the worship center in one accord? It's because the musicians take their cue from the concertmaster and not a standardized source. True unity cannot be obtained individually.

What happens if each musician decides to tune his or her instrument according to a separate standardized tone before entering the stage? Most likely, the resulting sound will not blend. Human ears have a tendency to tune on the high or low side of a note. With each musician tuning in isolation from the others, some will tend toward the high side, others the low side, and only some will hit the middle of the note. They need everyone on stage to tune all at once so they can find the point of perfect unity. Each musician has great individual talent, but as a group they must hear one another and blend for the sake of the entire orchestra.

Team sports often function the same way. A team must find a chemistry that allows its players to perform at their peak. They must learn to interact on an intuitive level. You can draft the best receiver available to complement your star quarterback, but if they can't anticipate and read each other's signals, the incomplete passes will drag the team down.

In team ministry, you need to tune yourself alongside

one another. You have to work at it until you get it right. And the next day, you will need to do it all over again.

Team Play

Sometimes many talented players can be teamed together, but they are unable to create teamwork. Whether due to personality and spiritual or theological differences, or whether due to a lack of balance among gifts and traits, there comes a time when the team must be revamped.

I recall a time when Dr. Evans came into a staff meeting and said, "Listen, we need to get everything ready for Vacation Bible School." But when the night before VBS came, nothing was ready. The team had bombed. People had misinterpreted information, and we had no teamwork. Our church has a talented staff, but at that point we were a sorry lot—a group of individuals doing their own thing rather than working together.

During the 2003–2004 NBA season, the Dallas Mavericks ran into a similar problem for awhile. They had drafted two great rookies, Josh Howard and Marquis Daniels. As the season continued, they traded several great players, Raef LaFrentz, Nick Van Exel, and others to gain Antawn Jamison, Antoine Walker, and Tony Delk. From the outside, it appeared these additions were better overall players for their system than the ones they had let go, but there was something they hadn't considered. Would these new players be able to weave themselves together to become a team and to understand who was playing what position?

Prior to the trades, Michael Finley, Dirk Nowitzki, and Steve Nash filled the star roles. Now, who would be the primary scorer? The secondary scorer? All of a sudden, everyone's role broke down, and they began wondering, *What is my new personality on this team?* For awhile, instead of increasing the team's success, the new players caused major mayhem because the team wouldn't glue. It just wouldn't come together.

Then at the end, Mavericks coach Don Nelson introduced "small ball." He used a smaller lineup with no extreme big men, justifying his decisions on their quickness and their ability to shoot and to score. This move brought the team together, and it brought a better philosophy to the Mavericks, putting all the personalities in their proper places so the team could become more balanced.

This problem occurs in the church as well. Sometimes the youth pastor, or the adult education pastor, or another associate leaves. And we think we can just fill in those spots with good position players. But it doesn't always work. The continuity between who does what and who is responsible for the work is lost. Not only did that associate vacate a written job description, but he also left behind an unwritten job description. Not only does his personality differ, but now the new pastor is following just the written job description, and the team doesn't mesh. Therefore, everybody has to readjust. It's no longer the same team.

When you lose experience, you lose many things that a team player person was doing to make his program successful. It's critical to check on those unwritten parts of the job description as you're making transitions. Most people didn't know the things I did just because I wanted the church to be better and because my experience gifted me with that ability. I could look at a situation and say, "This is going to cause us problems," because of my experience. I could check up on these problems before anyone else saw them.

On the other end, the new pastor must scale a huge wall of things yet to learn. As he's putting air between himself and the ground, what decisions will he make that will have eternal benefits and eternal disasters?

For example, he may make decisions that we will have to change in two years because we can't maintain the scope of the idea. Years ago, we told the congregation that if they would give us their Sundays and their Wednesdays, we would make them a church, and that's all that would be required of them. Now, twenty-nine years down the road, we need their Mondays, Tuesdays, Wednesdays, Thursdays, Fridays, Saturdays, Sundays, Mondays, Tuesdays, Wednesdays, Thursdays. . . . What we called part-time and volunteer jobs in the beginning have taken on a life of their own.

Now it's an unwritten law that people will have to be around here awhile to keep their jobs flowing. People have to come in just to do the work of the church. This happens especially when the church becomes large, yet we can't expect part-time staff and volunteers to work full-time. Therefore, sometimes we have to scale ministries down.

The learning curve for new staff members also includes realizing that their decisions are not single-person decisions, but much larger. For example, I did benevolence ministry from my office. When you have benevolence requests, you may honor it for one person because he deserves it. But the word will get around the church, and you will have to honor that situation for the rest of your life. So you have to ask yourself, "When I make this one move, can I make it with the next ten people? The next twenty people? And can I keep making this move?" It has a ripple effect, and the word *will* get out. Many people are so thankful that they just have to tell somebody how the church helped them.

When a new associate joins the team, the positions and job descriptions can be adjusted to match with the new team's overall design. Sometimes it takes more time than you think for everyone to hit the right note.

Team Play and Loyalty

So part of team play is staying with a team long enough for the individual personalities to gel—to find a philosophy like "small ball" that will best use each person's strengths for the greater good of the entire church. It's one thing for NBA teams to be trading players throughout the season; it's a different animal when you're talking about the church. Beyond having to readjust the players and cause the team to come together, loyalty becomes a huge issue within the church.

With loyalty comes trust. The more trustworthy you become, the more things people will trust you to do in the church—things that you can do where other people could not. So it's not only having the ability to do the ministry. A person can be an excellent administrator, but if nobody at the church trusts him, they don't want him in charge of the money. Or if they allow him to make decisions about the money, they will question his goals and objectives.

Once you become a loyal, trusted person within the church, it changes. The longer a person stays in a position, the higher his credibility status rises. Right now, assistants and associates are floating in and out every four years, three years, even two years. Instead of coming to a proper under-standing of God's value on their second chair ministry, they seek fulfillment by church hopping. They don't realize how big a toll that takes on their credibility.

I have several friends who were with me in Dallas who felt I should have been a senior pastor. One said, "Hawk, you've been called to be a pastor, and you ought to be ashamed of yourself for not doing that."

"That's a great statement," I told him, "but why doesn't God tell me that to the same degree that he's telling you? Why am I not convinced of that?"

"No, you should probably go back home to New Jersey and start a church there. You know that you're trained to do it, and it appears that's what God is calling you to do."

"That isn't as clear to me as it appears to be clear to you," I said. His knowledge of me is not equal to knowing God's will for my life. Yet I pondered his words.

Within a few years after that statement, he acknowledged that the hand of God was working in me at Oak Cliff Bible Fellowship. Perhaps both of my friends saw the obvious, yet overlooked the omnipotent hand of God in my life at my present calling. Both came to the conclusion that my stay at Oak Cliff Bible Fellowship was as much a God-ordained position as any I could have held.

Though other classmates had moved to several other churches, looking and seeking the "right fit," God had nestled me into a church home in which both the pastor and congregation recognized my skills and abilities. I was sure God's will for me was to remain where I was. Moving around has its benefits, giving opportunities to see ministry from multiple viewpoints. It also allows you to see your gifts used in a new environment and gives you a chance to evaluate yourself against a different team and staff.

Yet, staying and remaining in one place over a significant period of time helped me refine teamwork at a much deeper level of intimacy. Each associate pastor added to the staff brought a whole new dimension of administering, teaching, preaching, and caring that allowed us to build a highly motivated team of ministers. Whatever way God chooses to use you, having quality interpersonal skills rates high in creating God's successful team for your congregation.

Out of Balance

Other times, although you've hired gifted workers, the reality at your church doesn't recognize the equal calling of every minister. Distorted emphasis on one player—whether political, social, or financial—will pull everyone out of balance. When one team member, usually the senior pastor, receives compensation or recognition wildly out of scale with the rest of the team, the results can be dissension and an inability to employ quality teammates.

The Texas Rangers have been coping with this mistake. Attempting to build a championship team quickly, the Rangers management acquired Alex Rodriguez to play short-stop in 2001. He was a great player, but they signed him to a ten-year, $252 million contract.[1] Not only were they paying him out of scale with the rest of the players; they were paying him out of scale with the rest of the league. And the Rangers still continued to lose.

"A. Rod" may have been a wonderful player, and he played well while he was a part of the Rangers, but the team as a whole couldn't support him. The Rangers needed some younger arms, and the outfield needed to settle down, but they didn't have any money left to acquire those players. Worse than that, they slighted the wonderful players they already had. They lost Rafael Palmeiro and long-time and beloved catcher Ivan "Pudge" Rodriguez. The management's contract with A. Rod changed the nature of the Rangers from "Texas Rangers = team" to "Texas Rangers =

A. Rod." The last time I checked, it still takes nine players to win a baseball game.

How does this scenario affect the church? So often, the church name becomes synonymous with the senior pastor. And that's all right. Name recognition is good. It helps bring people into the ballpark. But think about the fact that the ratio of assistants and associates to the senior pastor at the average church lands somewhere around three or four to one. This means that the associates will have as much influence on the people as the pastor himself.

At our church, we have large groups of people working with outreach, large groups working with worship, large groups working with Christian education, and large groups working with administration and fellowship. You name an area—any area—and we have large groups of people working with the associate over that area. And that particular associate influences those members as much as anyone else in the church. So Dr. Evans gives his big vision. But then, the question becomes, how are these staff ministers going to carry out this vision, and how well?

The church that is gifted with a talented, godly senior pastor is blessed indeed—but not if the congregation emphasizes him so much, or the senior pastor values himself so much, that his salary and his recognition prohibits proper value being given to his staff. Just like the Rangers, that senior pastor might as well not have a staff. But either way, he'll experience losing seasons. The ministry does not consist of just one person.

By the same token, neither can the assistant pastor or a particular associate over worship or youth be treated as a star player. That star player can so dominate that he gets more of the attention. Before the A. Rod trade, the Rangers were bringing in new players for every season. But Rodriguez, by the nature of his experience and his notoriety, ended up influencing younger men and giving them loftier expectations. He was training them almost with his influence. His word became so dominant that the manager could not manage the team properly.

We had an unwritten law around our church that I as the assistant pastor should take care of the big funerals. When a high-profile funeral came up, Oak Cliff's involvement created a lot of implications, and in many cases I was appointed to oversee that funeral process. But I didn't oversee the funerals all the time, and sometimes that caused a bit of a rub. Without the right approach, the rest of the staff might have viewed me as the "star player." The pastor of comfort and care might have asked, "Why do you get to do that? Am I not good enough?"

This sort of thing can take the wind out of an associate's sails. We had good reason for doing it this way because in many of those cases I could speak for the church. I was given the authority to speak for the church for the most part unless it was something real bad going on. The pastor of care and comfort did not have that same authority. For example, if someone wanted to have a funeral at our church, but it was on a date that we already had something scheduled, I could ask the other group to switch the date. The pastor of care and comfort would have to say, "We don't have the date free." We lost some people who thought we didn't care when we told them they had to take their funeral or their wedding somewhere else.

But at the same time, we must communicate to the pastor of care and comfort that we recognize his ability and gifts for doing the funeral. In this case, the pastor had other reasons for putting me in as the designated hitter.

Now the Rangers have a group of young talent playing, and those guys are playing their hearts out. The team is doing better without A. Rod. It's the manager's team again, not A. Rod's team. Now they're winning with these rookies! Can you believe it? All these years with no rookies and no winning seasons. I believe the team had begun to say, "Let A. Rod do it. He's the star. He's being paid to win us games." Don't let that happen to your staff.

Who's the Coach?

Sometimes the discord comes not from theological or emotional differences but from politics. Churches have many different modes of government—congregational led, elder led, or pastor led, for example. When the leadership hierarchy becomes skewed—such as an elder who begins calling the shots in a pastor-led church—the resulting fouls cause a loss of game, no matter how hard the assistant tries to succeed. The same result occurs when the coach practices partiality politics.

Sometimes—although you've delineated the proper hierarchy of authority in the job description—the players in reality can become confused about the identity of their coach. As someone once said, "When church life is going well, no one is my boss; when church life is going badly, everyone is." People don't leave their opinions at the door when they enter the church. Everyone has an idea of how ministry should be run.

As senior pastors and assistant pastors, we should be listening to the needs of our congregations. But everyone involved must follow the established rules of authority—the chain of command—or it doesn't work. Conflict can rise to extreme levels when an assistant pastor who must answer to the senior pastor continues to hear from an elder, "Listen, I hired you. I need you to do this for me." Other times, the associate pastor must answer to an elder board, but the elder board won't allow that associate the freedom to support the senior pastor by bringing his specific ministry into line with the senior pastor's vision for the people.

Once again the beast of politics intimidates his way into controlling the ministry. The modern church uses many governmental models to do ministry. Who's to say which is right? Congregation led, elder led, or pastor led? I have my own opinion, but no definitive biblical mandate—except to say, let all that is done be done in love. And when it's not being done that way, someone needs to step in and make corrections.

Heeding the Umpire

When politics or tempers get out of hand, you must have an objective source to which to turn. The church constitution aids in mediation only when all parties agree on its meaning. Rather than resorting to secular courts as some churches have, a preestablished method of conflict resolution helps settle disagreements amiably and in accordance with 1 Corinthians 6.

- Always have a process that you can follow consistently.
- Give all parties an opportunity to speak without being interrupted.
- Ask questions about content.
- Be ready to talk to each person individually at times. We call this caucusing.
- Allow the Holy Spirit to weave it all together.
- Then make decisions based on truth.

A Good Trade

At the end of the day, your goal should be to keep the team together and restore unity. However, we sometimes find the spiritual chemistry just isn't there. Sometimes a team just cannot in all facets—theologically, emotionally, and practically—walk in one accord. The best solution for all involved in this situation is to trade and regroup.

Signals to Trade

- Unmanageable hours. Your required working hours remain consistently beyond what you—and more importantly, your family—can manage, in spite of your efforts to explain the problem to the leadership. (Make sure, however, that the fault and requirement lies in the leadership and not in your own workaholism.)

- Initial agreements ignored. You find that the leadership failed to disclose problems that you cannot reconcile in good faith. Or what was promised as you hired on failed to happen, and no one will discuss or acknowledge the discrepancies.

- Theological differences. What you believed to be the philosophy of the church or senior pastor drastically changed, or your theology changed and can no longer support the church's viewpoint.

- Irreconcilable personalities or difference. You find that your relationship with the senior pastor has become so uncomfortable that others are beginning to see the conflict and friction between you.

A Change in Management

Eventually, the senior pastor will retire or move to a new calling. What does this mean for the staff? I'd like to say that the new senior pastor can work with the old staff—I'd pray that he could. Sometimes when the new senior pastor was already at the church as an unintentional assistant like Joshua, the team can remain. But because of personalities, the change often just doesn't work. The senior pastor must have a staff that can work with him and implement his vision.

The new senior pastor's vision will not look exactly like the previous pastor's. It can't—because of its ties to the previous pastor's individual gifts and design. Ralph Abernathy was Martin Luther King's second chair. Martin Luther King led a worldwide march. He shared his vision with the world. When King died, Abernathy took over, and he said, "We're going to keep on with Martin's dream." But that was Martin's dream, not Ralph's. Abernathy couldn't lead someone else's dream; he needed to lead his own. So instead of Martin Luther King's dream continuing as it was, and instead of Abernathy rising to the same prominence in leading the march, young men like Jesse Jackson, who translated the dream into their own visions, came to the forefront of the movement.

When the coach leaves, natural attrition often takes place. Associate pastors will need to expect this possibility.

Aiming for Harmony

Whether a parting of ways occurs because of irreconcilable differences or because of a change in management, we should always be aiming for harmony and effective ministry. Even firing should be done in harmony. If God is in the relationship and in the church, and if these two people are mature, it should be that we're sending them to something better. Like the A. Rod–Soriano trade, the move should benefit both teams and both players. A. Rod fits better with the Yankees. They can handle his caliber. When it doesn't work, it doesn't mean that it's been a failure; it just means that this isn't the venue God has for you to work at this time.

The person in the second chair should be the person who is best for that job. If you aren't or can't be the best, it may be time to find out where God is calling you next. On the other hand, if you are the best person for the job, and you are troubled by discord, perhaps you haven't used your resources for reconciliation.

Chapter Eight

Restoring Harmony

Now to Him who is able to do far more abundantly beyond
all that we ask or think, according to the power that works
within us, to Him be the glory in the church and in Christ
Jesus to all generations forever and ever. Amen
(Eph. 3:20–21)

*A*s I settled and grew into my role as assistant pastor,
I found joy in using my creative juices to cause people to
visit the church, to come to the church, to want to stay at
the church. The church grew larger, and I set up a system
called Care Cells. We divided people initially into four
major groups—geographically located—that we could
care for in a minichurch kind of way. I believe Gene Getz
pioneered the concept, but we modified it to meet our
own needs.

Care Cells were my "baby," and I felt like they answered all of our spiritual, political, and compassion needs. We could call red alerts within a particular cell, quickly access the members of the community, and mobilize forces to take care of the needs of our members. Creating these groups within geographical areas made the best sense to me. It helped the people in that location get to know each other and minister to one another.

Then one day, Dr. Evans informed the staff that we were going to do something different. The Care Cells would be dissolved—just like that. I disagreed with his decision in every pore of my being.

Necessary Tension

Every church will experience times of tension. In musical terms, a good composition is not one that has sweet, unchallenged tones throughout. Instead, the composer purposefully sets the notes into an occasionally discordant structure as a driving force that moves toward a harmonic resolution. That makes good music. Constant discord gives you no rest, but a melody without any tension, is, well, boring.

Every church staff will experience tension. It is not the lack of tension or discordant times that makes a good staff; it is their ability to move consistently to the harmonic resolution.

The "How" of Unity

What makes the difference between a staff that has to trade players and one that can find resolution? The Holy Spirit. From each person understanding his calling to each person valuing the other's worth under heaven, restoring harmony always involves the Holy Spirit. Harmony requires humility. And true humility depends on the Holy Spirit.

Did you wonder a couple of chapters ago how you were going to turn communication into comradeship—especially with your current senior pastor or your current associate? How were you going to get past all the misunderstanding and "bad blood" already between you? This is it. Listen up.

Submitting to One Another

Ephesians 5:18 commands us to "be filled with the Spirit." What does being "filled" look like? Paul describes it as "speaking to one another in psalms and hymns and spiritual songs, singing and making melody with your heart to the Lord; always giving thanks for all things in the name of our Lord Jesus Christ to God, even the Father" (Eph. 5:19–20). Being filled with the Spirit means having the peace and contentment—whatever our situation, whatever our position—to recognize that all we have, even our relationship to God the Father, comes from Jesus' work on our behalf. The work of the second chair. It was the Father's perfect vision to give his Son for us, but it was the Son's perfect work that accomplished the goal.

"And," Paul adds, it includes being "subject to one another in the fear of Christ" (Eph. 5:21). Being filled with the Spirit includes submitting our wills to one another out of reverence to Christ.

I've read that passage in Ephesians for years and yet wondered about the "how." *How* does one submit himself to another? After much study, I've concluded that Paul answers that question back in chapter 4 when he says, "with all humility and gentleness, with patience, showing forbearance to one another in love, being diligent to preserve the unity of the Spirit in the bond of peace" (Eph. 4:2–3). We submit to one another to preserve the unity of the Spirit. You will have unity if you abide by these four main principles. I want you to be humble, I want you to be meek, I want you to be patient, and I want you to bear with one another. There is no way a person can attack you when you're doing these four things. Even if the person is angry, he will succumb when you respond humbly, "I can see this is bothering you a lot." And then you listen with meekness, where you are showing, "It's not important what I feel right now; it's important what you feel." And you add patience and long-suffering to the mix to say, "Hey, I'm not going to get angry and all riled up with this thing. I'm just going to watch and see how the Lord works this thing with you."

And it must be done "in love." We are to fulfill these four principles of walking in the Spirit in love, and we are to speak the truth in love (Eph. 4:15). In love, you add humility, meekness, patience, and forbearance to speaking the truth with grace. Humility and meekness say, "I just got zinged by you, but it's OK." And gracefulness zings it around to the other side and says, "How can I build you up with that?" And the building up says, "Wow, I must have really hurt you if you said that to me. Forgive *me* for making you come at me that way. I know you wouldn't have reacted that way without reason." This is the art of unity—in humility, meekness, patience, and forbearance speaking the truth in love and grace, we leave nothing on the table for anger to grab.

And when we go all the way back to Ephesians 4:1, we see Paul not just commanding us to walk with harmony and unity, but begging us: "I, therefore, the prisoner of the Lord, entreat you to walk in a manner worthy of the calling with which you have been called." Now Paul is speaking of the calling on all believers to live worthy of the predestination, adoption, and glory of God's riches bestowed on us from eternity past. But he also speaks in this chapter of persons set aside as pastors, as leaders. If *every* believer should walk in unity, submitting themselves in the Spirit to one another, how much more should we as *leaders* model this behavior? Walking in unity is not a suggestion; it is a command. And it is how we restore harmony as we tighten the strings in our tuning process.

Choosing God's Battle Lines

Yes, I disagreed with dissolving the Care Cells. They were a part of my vision for the church. But they were no longer a part of Dr. Evans's vision. I had to be humble about something so important to me because the philosophy of the church belonged in the hands of the senior pastor. Although his idea differed from mine, his had just as much merit because they were both just ideas, not biblical mandates.

When it's a matter of biblical principle, stand. When it's a matter of personal preferences, yours is as good as mine even though I think mine's best. When you are choosing battle lines, make sure that the ones God has chosen are the only ones you choose for yourself. I disagreed, but it wasn't God's battle line. So I allowed my idea to be "punched down" for the sake of Christ. I realigned myself with Dr. Evans's vision. I fulfilled my calling and kept harmony between us.

Make Bread to Break Bread

I'm no cook, but from what I've read about making bread, I know this: you need flour, you need other ingredients, you need leaven, and you need time. Now no one says, "Bread is made of salt." But salt needs to be in there for flavor. No one says, "Bread is made of water, milk, or egg." But these are the binding agents that hold the loaf together. No one says, "Bread is made of leaven." But if you want a light loaf that's easy to chew, you need it.

People say, "Bread is made from flour." Yes. And the flour is the senior pastor—he's the main ingredient that most people acknowledge and remember. But bread is not made from flour alone. It is essential, but it is not the whole loaf. The salt, the binding agent, and the other creative flavorings that make up a particular kind of bread are just as important. They are the staff—the associates, the assistants, and the volunteers. And the leavening is the Holy Spirit.

To create a fine loaf, the Good Baker will mix all the individual ingredients and then allow the leavening to do its work. Then, the Baker punches down the dough. He kneads it to mix it and bind it together, and he punches it down to get rid of any inflated ideas, any empty air bubbles. He must really punch it and work the dough hard. If he skips this step, the result will have huge holes. Then the Baker lets it rise again. He lets the Holy Spirit work. More than once, the Baker takes his dough through this process, perfecting its texture and appearance.

Finally, after much time, the Baker puts the loaf into the oven to bake. When the ingredients have been measured and mixed well, when they have endured the kneading and the punching, when they have been multiplied by the work of the leavening, a delicious aroma rises from the pan—and no one will be able to distinguish one ingredient from another. The loaf will have a uniform appearance and will be light and fluffy from the Holy Spirit's work, ready to melt in the mouth of those who eat it.

It's Not Easy

Whether we're in outreach, music and worship, administration, or education, our job—our calling—is to support the pastor in unity, in harmony, and with the sweet aroma of the Holy Spirit. We must blend with him until all the ingredients look as one. And you know if you're already there—*it's not easy!* We must endure much kneading and punching down. We must allow the Holy Spirit into the pan to do his work. And even then, not only is it not easy, but those who benefit from the whole loaf will say, "It was made of flour."

But still, creating the loaf is worth the effort. If we truly welcome the Holy Spirit into the whole mix, if with humility we allow the Baker to punch us all down a few times, our one loaf can feed the five thousand.

Weaving Us Together

Occasionally, Dr. Evans has a tendency to forget things. (Who doesn't?) One Saturday, he was going to perform a wedding that I was attending but not participating in. We have worked together so much and bonded in brotherhood so much that I knew he was going to forget the portable communion tray. Halfway there, I doubled all the way back, and found the communion tray.

The first thing he said when I walked into the worship center was, "Do you have the communion tray?" I brought the communion tray in, gave it to him, and he said, "How did you know to bring this?" I told him, "I figured it out coming down here. I said to myself that Dr. Evans is going to forget the communion tray, and I picked it up and put it in my car because I knew you'd need it." It was the Holy

Spirit guiding us in the same direction, so that we could complement each other.

The Spirit of God has a responsibility in weaving us together. How we help the senior pastor most is by performing our jobs well, producing and having a vision within his vision. The pastor gives us a vision, but we put it on paper so he can see what our vision is within his vision. Then all the ministry can begin instead of us having to wait for him to initiate everything before we jump. Over time you blend with the Holy Spirit's help, and you begin to know the habits of the senior pastor so much that you almost think before he does, and so you can get some things accomplished before he directs it. I don't normally think to go get the communion tray, but that Saturday it was the Spirit of God who led me to do so.

The Warts of Humanity

The truth of the matter is that relationships take work. If you're looking for the perfect place to work in terms of everyone getting along easily—you won't find it. You'll always find dissension in some form or another either on the staff, the board, or among the congregation. God is bringing us all along on this journey called life, knocking out the kinks and sin as we go.

Knowing the academics of ministry, being sharp in theology, these are good things. But when it comes to academics versus attitude, I'll take attitude every time—an attitude of humility brought about by the Holy Spirit.

Without humility, even pastors who enter the profession because they care about the people turn into prima donnas. They might think, *I'm not going to do this unless it's a certain way.* My answer to this is, you need to minister, just minister. Take it the way it is, and then take it the way it needs to go. That's all you do. We don't need to know how skilled you are. We need to know, *Can you minister?* Can you minister to your staff? Can you minister to the congregation? Can you minister to me? In spite of me? With all my bumps and warts, can you be effective and love me? Humility always answers *yes.*

It Works through the Holy Spirit

We are equal in calling, but not in position. We are equal in worth, but not in position. We are equal in labor, but not in position. The senior pastor has the authority. It's God-given. I pray for every associate—that your senior pastor will recognize and appreciate your humility. I pray for every assistant—that your congregation will notice your constant service and diligence. But we are called to such *regardless* of earthly notice. It's not easy. But it can happen when you are filled with Holy Spirit. Your ministry will depend on how much you allow the Spirit to do his work in you.

Chapter Nine

Worn Strings:
Understanding and
Protecting Your Needs

*But he himself went a day's journey into the wilderness,
and came and sat down under a juniper tree; and he
requested for himself that he might die, and said, "It is
enough; now, O LORD, take my life, for I am not better
than my fathers." And he lay down and slept under a
juniper tree; and behold, there was an angel touching him,
and he said to him, "Arise, eat." Then he looked and
behold, there was at his head a bread cake baked on hot
stones, and a jar of water. So he ate and drank and lay
down again. And the angel of the LORD came again a
second time and touched him and said, "Arise, eat, because
the journey is too great for you." So he arose and ate and
drank, and went in the strength of that food forty days and
forty nights to Horeb, the mountain of God.*
(1 Kings 19:4–8)

*A*llowing the Spirit to work in you and the rest of the ministry team will also help prevent ministry burnout. Maybe you haven't reached burnout—perhaps you just have strings that are smoking from the constant, incessant bow rubbing against them. But every minister, whether first, second, third, or fourth chair, needs to be aware of this danger. It can start as a misperception about your worth or the worth of others. It can start as a sincere desire to do the most you possibly can for God's kingdom by way of the church. It can even start as the result of your giftedness. But it always ends the same way—discouragement, disgruntlement, and disloyalty. Beware. Satan knows how to use ministry—and humankind's fallen response to ministry—to further his agenda.

A Congregation in the Cemetery

There are many times—probably more times than we care to admit—when the congregation just doesn't seem to care. Senior pastors make jokes about members holding their eyelids open with toothpicks during the sermon or not having a clue what he talked about last week or last night or last hour. Preachers can do their job well, extremely well, and still, most of the hearers have moved on to more "important" things in their lives soon after the benediction. We need to realize that going in as ministers.

One professor I know used to take his preaching class to the cemetery every semester to preach and call out believers from under the gravestones. He wanted to make the point, of course, that many of the people to which they would be ministering would be just as deaf to their preaching as those already dead and buried in the cemetery. It takes God's act of resurrecting new life in believers for ministry to be able to grab hold of people and shake the dirt off.

Wearing Down

How do we fall prey to burnout? Like any job, some of the day-to-day work can become monotonous. And often, the results of what we do as ministers cannot be seen on paper or with earthly eyes. Without recognition of our work or timely, tangible evidence that we're accomplishing God's will in people, we sometimes begin to wonder whether it's all worth the effort.

If the senior pastor can find so much discouragement in his inability to reach the people, in their criticism of his preaching the real truth, in the endless task of meeting needs, how much more easily can the second chair fall to resentment when he finds that the congregation—and maybe even the senior pastor as well—has no appreciation for the hard work he does. Many times the congregation thinks the assistant exists just to please the pastor. They don't realize the actual work that is being done.

I'm at a good church, but I have to admit that there are maybe twenty people in the entire body who know what I did as the assistant pastor. Part of that is not explaining it to the members well, but part of it is that as soon as you give the initial explanation, it may change. People can't keep up with the ministries I was responsible for and those in which I was not involved. They might have suspected that if they needed benevolence funds or reconciliation, they should go to Pastor Hawkins. They did know me for my leadership role at Oak Cliff, but they didn't know everything I was responsible for and the extent to which I administered those duties.

You might think that associates over specific ministries would receive some recognition. After all, their titles usually "explain" their ministries. But consider the associate for Christian education. He does all the education all the time. Everybody just takes it for granted that the courses will be there. For five years, all they have had to do is come and sign out the materials. They don't know how hard he had to think and plan to get those materials ready.

Or he might have set up different levels of courses. He tied into external learning organizations, like universities, that give credit. He made sure that he has all the correct arrangements and that people are getting credit for the work they do. They don't have a clue how those agreements work or what went into scheduling them. All the members do in many cases is just enjoy the fruits of his hard work.

The music ministry is another good example. Worship pastors must find fresh music every week. At the same time, they must tune in to the policy, the polity, and the politics of the church because you are never able to have music that pleases everybody. You have the older group that usually wants to hear more hymns of the faith. The younger people want praise songs that have more meaning for them. The worship pastor has to perform a delicate balance. The members who have been at the church for a long time are the main financial givers. If he doesn't please them, they're going to pull out. Yet, he also wants to reach new people for Christ.

Not only do worship pastors live that headache; they must stay the long hours teaching the music to the orchestra, teaching it to the praise team, and teaching it to the choir so everyone can enjoy it on Sunday. Little do people know that they stay at the church often from 6:00 in the afternoon to 11:00 or 12:00 at night making sure everything is right. Making sure the stage is right. Making sure the speaker system doesn't go down, or doesn't cause reverb when someone sings a solo. He stays there half the night— and then the microphone doesn't work for the first solo. He begins to think, *What's all this for?*

And of course youth pastors not only have to work with staff authority; they must contend with parents of every sort and with every sort of opinion. Yet somehow, they manage to actually teach the young people something about Christ. Generally, the youth pastor can't win for winning. He decides to take the youth on an incredible missions trip, and then the bus breaks down. The parents get angry. Or it's delayed beyond his control so that where their arrival time was supposed to be at 6:00 p.m., now they are delayed until 10:00 p.m. Thus the wonderful experience that the youth have encountered becomes overshadowed with whining and criticism for the associate's imperfect bus—the bus that he contracted to save the parents the need to drive. He just never seems to win.

Are you discouraged yet? What about the people who are responsible for outreach, evangelism, or missions? These missionaries have been there long years. The congregation doesn't ask about them, and sometimes they view mission week as an imposition on the church. "Why do we have to hear about missions for a whole month?" they complain. "Why do we need to have mission priorities?" People struggle to understand its importance.

And when we have evangelism, nobody wants to visit at night, going door to door. They want to hear about all these people coming to Christ, but they're not sure they want to do it. They want more innovative ways to evangelize than door knocking, but again they're not willing to work on the innovative ways. When the outreach pastor calls for volunteers to help with evangelism, only a faithful few usually show up.

Maybe all this discussion has you wanting to be an administrative pastor, so you don't have to work so much with people. Try again. In administration, you have to put the schedule of rooms and equipment together. You get the room all put together, and the people say, "I didn't want it that way." Or you spend months developing a budget only to find it not properly balanced, in the opinion of some people.

It's discouraging sometimes. Many associate pastors can feel discouraged. You give four or five years of service, and you begin to feel that this work is getting to be a little bit much. Understanding your calling becomes remote. Your good work is often taken for granted, and the congregation doesn't appreciate what goes into creating a good ministry. Their expectation of you is so high, it's as if you're little gods. Letters come in about what you failed to accomplish, but you rarely see letters of encouragement. Rarely do people give an accolade about an excellent program. They expect that. Yet you need encouragement as well. These are the little things that drag you down. This, too, is part of ministry.

Never-ending Need

And with all you do, you also have to minister to the people. Someone is always sick or dying and needing crisis attention. Your being there is everything. Your love for the people will often cause people to call on you all the time. For example, we recently had a member going into surgery. While seeing him, my former worker had a recurring lupus attack. I'm her pastor. Even though she's not working for me anymore, the first person she expects to see is me. So now I've got two to visit in the hospital. And while I'm visiting those two, I hear from a member I've known for a long time. Her mother is dying and is in another room right around the corner. When I go to see the mother, she's already in a comatose state.

When I get back to the church, the daughter of that mother who is dying is asking me, "What do I do to set up funeral arrangements." So I tell her the best places and various details and talk about costs. And then in the midst of that conversation, we get a call from someone else.

It's never-ending. Do I sound callous? I love the people. I want to help them, and it's all ministry that I signed up for. It's good work. But it's draining. It's emotional. It's long hours, and it never ends.

And on top of that, you have doctrinal or personal issues and social issues. Perhaps somebody is being sexually molested. Perhaps a member reports that one of the ushers who walked her to the car touched her inappropriately. You've got to work these things out in your ministry. You've got to make sure that everyone is held accountable. And you have to address this person wanting to leave the church because she feels like the harassment isn't being dealt with.

You do your best to give and give to the people. You perform benevolence, but sometimes you have to reject people's requests. Then many come back and say to you, "You were unfair in your judgments." And you have to say to them, "We're trying to create financial and spiritual accountability." These are the issues of serving a growing church.

A Theo-Ego

As ministers, we can't let the ministry work us to the point that we're the ones lying in the casket because we've stressed ourselves out to the point of death. If we're in the casket, then we've elevated ourselves with a theo-ego, a God complex. Sometimes I envision myself lying up front, and then sitting up in the casket and saying, "No, I didn't die because the Lord was ready for me; I died because I tried to meet all of your needs!" I had better reassess who I think I am and what I'm doing when I begin to feel that way.

We can't meet all the needs of the people; God can. We aren't available 24/7; God is. But we love each member, and we love the job in spite of the challenges and problems. The congregation's needs will be there; we, as ministers, must learn to protect our own needs and health while serving.

It's All the Little Things

Andrew Pryor attributes the following symptoms to a discouraged ministry: "preoccupation with money"—or truly, the lack of it; "let down"—a lack of motivation and effort; "feverish activity"—working beyond all reasonable limits trying to get someone to notice; and being "distracted by extracurriculars"—pursuing outside rewards and avenues to the detriment of your job.[1] If you find yourself battling these symptoms, you need to step back and evaluate. You need to follow Jesus up on the mountain to pray, away from the people and the pressure.

Rarely does a principled, practiced, praying minister just fall off a cliff and create a big scandal. It was all the little things in his life that he allowed to push him slowly toward the chasm.

Falling off the Cliff

Burnout will lead to sin—maybe not the big ones at first. But how do you think so many harvest workers have fallen into adultery? Satan knows your weaknesses. Satan knows your need for encouragement and recognition. He's got a woman in the wings just waiting—waiting for you to quit finding your worth and recognition in God's eyes, waiting for you to quit finding your encouragement in your wife's arms, and waiting for you to start finding a shallow version of what you need in this other woman.

Listen up. I don't care how discouraged you feel, or how welcoming she seems—*don't go there.* Don't ever allow your weariness or your theo-ego to send you there. You're better off running away like Elijah did from Jezebel's wrath; let God bolster you up. Because if you run to that accommodating woman instead, her fulfillment of your ego and your emotional needs will be a puddle compared to the bottomless pit you'll find yourself in spiritually, relationally, and professionally. Most ministries won't counsel you or pull you out of the pit. Most wives won't endure it either. They'll just leave you there, look over the edge, and say, "Shame on you, you've fallen." One or two ministries out there will restore a fallen pastor, but not most. Don't go there.

As humans, we've all got closets both big and small that cause us to think we should give up the ministry. We know the sin we have in our lives, yet people are looking at us as if we're on a spiritual pedestal. Satan is just waiting for you to believe that you're worthless—and then he'll lead you farther down a worthless path. The sin in our lives should keep us humble and keep us on our knees before God. When we fail to keep the unity, when we do less than we want, we need the humility (there it is again) to say, "I can't do it all, but I can fall on the grace of God and let him work through me."

Fellow Mountaineers

And with humility, too, we need to surround ourselves with accountability partners who are for real. If you want to minister, if you want to be on the front lines of the spiritual battle, you need to act like a mountain climber who ties himself to other good mountaineers so they can hold him up when he starts to slip. I'm not talking about fifteen men who won't ask the hard questions. I'm talking about someone who, with love, will come chest to chest with you, eyeball to eyeball, and ask, "Did you watch pornography last night? Did you go out with her last night? Did you gamble last night?"

There's a group of men around me who are superb. Two or three are elders who have grown very close to me over the years. One of them calls me up almost every day to ask, "What are you doing?" And if I don't call him back, he says, "Well, you're a big shot now, not calling little old me anymore." He's a good friend. Along with those elders, I have some men on my board at Metro Discipling Ministries. They'll tell me everything. They'll say to me, "Pastor, you're a little strung out—you're doing five, six things. Calm down." And I'll answer, "Well, I'm only doing six. The average man should be able to do ten." They keep me going, and they keep me honest with myself.

Maintain Your Instrument

When you find yourself in need of new strings, you first have to regain your focus. If you're going to remain in the orchestra, you must focus on the reason why you're here. That takes the Word of God. Find time for your own personal Bible study so you can remember that *God has sent you here for a purpose.* Second, focus on the idea that since he sent you here for a purpose, *let him fulfill that purpose in your lifetime.* Work hard toward fulfilling that as opposed to just meeting your own needs.

Third, you need to add to your Bible reading *much prayer,* and even more prayer. I've read somewhere that people who pray more than an average of one and one-half hours per day are more successful than those who pray only half an hour per day. Whatever prayer life you have, increase it, because while this discouragement could be a result of your flesh, it could also be an attack from Satan.

Just because you're in the ministry, the order of priorities does not change. *The church is not the number-one priority in your life; God is.* God himself, he's first. Second, you need to value your family. If you get fired or relieved of your job, who's going to hurt the most? Those who are closest to you. So spend time with them. *Then* think of your church work. Say to yourself, "I will work the long hours when it's needed, but I will also raise up other people who can handle just as well as I can some of the problems that occur."

We've got to take time for our wives and children. Many pastors have lost their lives and their ministries trying to satisfy the people—when the people they should be satisfying the most are their own families.

In your job description, you should have discussed what realistic working hours looked like. Are you sticking with the plan? Probably not, if you're like most ministers. How are your wife and your children accepting your work schedule? Is your wife distressed? Is she hinting that your job is taking on a life of its own?

When was the last time you took a vacation? Not a planning retreat—a vacation with your family? How does your wife feel about the security of your job? Usually, I've discovered, wives have a better sense of when the church leadership is about to ask an associate to find a new position. Are you concerned about money at home but afraid to ask for a raise? All these little details can turn one day of discouragement into months of battle fatigue.

Once you regain your focus, you should take some action to keep your life and your work well maintained. Even when the relationship between the senior pastor and the assistant falls short of the ideal, the following suggestions can keep your ministry strong.

First, protect your time with God. Second, protect your time with your family. Third, Chris Smith in "Sweet Music from a Second Fiddle" suggests asking to take on some responsibilities "that earn congregational appreciation and admiration: preaching, hospital calling, home visitation, weddings, and funerals" to balance out all those jobs that "are often the source of criticism and disapproval: youth programs, Christian education, social action, evangelism, and ministry to young adults."[2] He says, "If you are a youth minister, beg to teach an adult class. If you work with single adults, offer to do some hospital calling. If you are the Christian education minister, ask to do some weddings. Working in a few winning areas will increase your influence and make ministry more interesting."[3]

Get back to your passion. Communicate with the leadership of the church so you can spend more of your week working on tasks that energize you rather than drain you. Discuss a change in hours, if needed. Schedule regular vacations. Charles T. Hindman makes these suggestions:

1. Interpret the role yourself. Make sure *you* can explain what you do even if it's only to say, "I do

everything the other pastor does, only in different amounts."

2. Grow in the role, using strengths. Focus on what is working and what is possible.

3. Don't defeat yourself. Self-esteem and identity must not be based on besting the senior pastor, gaining any one person's approval, or influencing a decision to go your way. Like Rodney Dangerfield, associates can become so worried about not being respected that their fear becomes a self-fulfilling prophecy.

4. Develop informal power. Ultimately, power to minister comes from developing gifts and graces, nurturing relationships, and fostering a sense of the spiritual. Any minister is able to work at these informal sources of power, no matter what the senior-associate relationship.

5. Develop your spiritual resources.[4]

Remember the Advantages

As second chair, rather than complain about the struggles and challenges, remember the advantages of not being the senior pastor. When you're enjoying fellowship with your family or church members on a Saturday night, remind yourself that you could be sitting behind a desk until the wee hours finishing tomorrow's sermon. When a church member asks to speak to the pastor, but finding him not in, goes home instead of speaking to you, remind yourself that there are many sticky issues that you get to pass on to his plate. Being second can be an opportunity to grow without all the frontline pressure.

Helping Each Other

And as I've mentioned before, the attitude of the senior pastor plays a huge role in the success of his team. Hidden behind the senior pastor, assistant pastors tend to mask feelings of low self-esteem, poor self-image, and personal frustration. There are times they might compare themselves with the senior pastor: sometimes desiring his success and wanting a larger "piece of the pie." If the associate has little authority, he might feel emptiness and a lack of self-confidence with overbearing life issues. Pastoral care also includes taking care of your co-laborers. The senior pastor who dares to be different can identify these special times and create opportunities for encouragement.

Before the Congregation

While encouragements may be family to family or senior pastor to assistant and mostly private, encourage-ment before the congregation is one of the greatest ego builders for assistants who need shoring up. The senior pastor's spending personal time, his being sensitive to spe-cial needs, and his creating an open climate for communication can also rescue a falling assistant from self-pity. It takes senior pastors with the keen eye of the Holy Spirit and with the wisdom of Solomon, using skillfulness of prayer and experience, to minister to the assistant's need, which is one of assurance. Balancing the Word with the tender touch of caring will accomplish more than any well-wishers who offer only glib statements such as "hang in there."

At the same time, the assistant should be working hard to keep the senior pastor from going over the edge. When the lead minister knows that his staff can and will follow through, he becomes free to pursue *his* passion in ministry. We must remember that encouragement is a two-way street.

Chapter Ten

Second Fiddle to the Second Fiddle: Did They Hire Your Wife?

She opens her mouth in wisdom,
And the teaching of kindness is on her tongue.
She looks well to the ways of her household,
And does not eat the bread of idleness.
(Prov. 31:26–27)

$\mathcal{I}$ hope by now you have started to understand the position of the associate as second chair and not as second fiddle. Now let's take a moment to consider your wife. Is she your second chair? Or your second fiddle?

Be honest with yourself. No one's looking. No one knows what you're reading at the moment. Do you consider her needs to have as much priority as yours? Or do your needs have priority because your ministry brings the bread home? Do you allow her to sit as copilot? Do you let her help navigate your journey with her counsel? Or do you just toss her in the backseat with the kids and bring her along for the ride?

Just as the associate pastor deserves to be recognized as the best man for his job, your wife needs to be honored for the way she fills her role with all her gifts and skills. She may be different. She may do things and see things differently. That's OK. Believe me, you wouldn't want to be married to another *you.*

Some of you in the ministry may find yourselves, right now, resenting your wife. Why? Because she doesn't have the passion for ministry like you do. She doesn't understand your hours. She doesn't volunteer. She doesn't reach out to others easily like you. You have to drag her along to functions and insist she sing in the choir or attend the women's retreat. She hints at wanting to do something else whenever the ladies' auxiliary club needs people to serve. In other words, she's not living up to your idea of a pastor's wife.

Well, I have a few words for you. When the church signed you on, it was a contract for one. They did not hire your wife—or your family—as assistant pastor.

Contract for One

Often a church will hire a pastor and expect that his wife and kids are a part of the deal. If the wife can play the piano, she'll be counted on to fill that slot. Or perhaps the youth pastor's wife will feel obligated to help chaperone every retreat.

The kids, too, will be expected to be better than everyone else's and to participate in all facets of the youth ministry. That's a huge problem for PKs because they already feel the pressure of that expectation—and then if the church confirms that requirement in how they treat those children—well, we might as well just set up a therapy fund right now. Not too long ago, my daughter Melissa told me, "Dad, I don't mind you telling people that I'm a preacher's kid, but let people accept me for me, and *then* you tell them I'm a PK. Because sometimes what I do may not match up with their expectations."

It would be good for the church to stop placing such pressure on a minister's family. But ultimately, it must be up to that minister to protect his family and relieve that pressure.

Giving Your Wife Freedom

The assistant must stand as the steel wall between the church and his wife. Some wives will desire to participate and volunteer as the Holy Spirit leads them, but the steel wall must ensure that such participation is always an expression of service and joy in the Lord rather than a fulfillment of her obligation.

You need to know the personality of your wife. You need to know what will fill her up and what will drain even her reserves. My wife loves to work. If we had twenty million dollars, she would still love to do what's she's doing. As director of training at the Dallas Independent School District, she is not only a good trainer, but a great trainer. And when she comes home, she has tireless energy to perform the loving tasks of planting flowers in the yard and cooking great meals. Even when our daughter was little I told my wife, "You've only got one small child now. She's right around the corner, and I've got the freedom of time to be called on. I can be there in a second." Eventually Melissa went to our school next door to the church, and I was right nearby—although I imagine there were times she wished I wasn't.

You may agree or disagree with our arrangement, but I'm not asking your opinion. And that's the point. As a family, we decided what was best for us, what fit our situation and allowed us to come together to be all that we could be. We didn't let the church dictate what Shirley should be doing every minute of the day. We didn't consider her an unpaid employee—an indentured servant by virtue of marriage. Although I'm sure at times I could have used her extra hands to accomplish tasks at the church, I had to recognize, with humility, her design and the chair that God had called her to fill.

My wife isn't my second fiddle—someone wanting to be me but not quite good enough yet. She's my second chair, complementing my life with her unique gifts and design while fitting her vision into the scope of my vision and leadership.

Freedom to Serve

I didn't know it for a long time, but at some point Shirley began going through the bulletin every week and sending cards to the sick. Eventually, people started coming to me saying, "Thanks for your card." That's how I found out she was doing this. It's a tremendous ministry. Maybe it doesn't seem like a lot, but it gives people a warm touch just when they need it. It tells them they matter. I've admired Shirley for taking the time to send those cards—and not because she had to, or because she was the assistant's wife. She did it from a heart of caring for the congregation. She did it from her passion for the Lord.

My wife will have people over to our house from time to time. She'll bake bread that the staff and friends look forward to. But it all comes from her heart of giving and not from expectation. I think that has helped her stick with me in the ministry for the long haul and not resent my hours and the demands of the people.

Beating Down the Stereotypes
The Assistant's Wife

Both from the congregation at large and the church leadership family, the assistant's wife will encounter many preconceived expectations. Let us learn to honor the assistant's wife by not obligating her to ministry that she didn't sign up for, that she's not designed for, or that keeps her from her rightful calling. Let us also include her as an equal alongside the senior pastor's wife, as one in need of encouragement and spiritual care.

The Single Minister

And while we are honoring our wives, let's not look down on single associates either. Too often, especially because a church wants what a wife can offer them, a congregation is too concerned about a single pastor's marital status. Being single can benefit an associate by giving him more freedom with his time and schedule to do the ministry. (On the other hand, the single man must still remember to guard personal time for himself. He will find this more difficult than his married counterpart because he will probably be "programmed" to consider self time as selfish, unlike family time.)

Granted, a single minister will lack personal experience when it comes to counseling couples and the relationship maturity that comes with the marriage journey. He will also have to pay close attention to the unintentional signals he sends to females within the church and to how and when he pursues a courtship. But he should not allow the church to undermine his ability to minister or his effectiveness. Like the second chair assistant, the single pastor is designed for a specific place and a specific calling—and he has many biblical and historical models to follow.

Chapter Eleven

Whittling a Fiddle into a Brass Horn

Before I formed you in the womb I knew you, and
before you were born I consecrated you; I have appointed
you a prophet to the nations. (Jer. 1:5)

 o you know your calling? Do you understand your passion for ministry? What purpose has God given you that will be your life's work to fulfill? It comes down to that—to those simple but lifelong discovery questions.

Maintaining a fulfilling and effective ministry as an assistant or associate pastor comes down to asking and answering this question: Is this the role God has for me? Can I serve him faithfully in this capacity and build his kingdom? Despite all that I have outlined up to now, about the traits, needs, and strategies for the assistant pastor, despite all the years that I have seen these things proven true, God remains sovereign. For his purposes, he lets the weakest concertmaster play the most valuable violin or causes the most mismatched pair to become a beautiful duet.

The Unintentional Intentional Assistant: The Martin Hawkins Effect

I've already told you that I thought I would become a senior pastor. What I haven't said is that in many of the aspects that I've discussed, my design fits as a *senior* pastor—and yet I enjoyed year upon year as an assistant. I found my passion and my calling within that role. I might not have found my passion at a different church; I might not have found my calling with a different senior pastor; but at Oak Cliff Bible Church with Dr. Tony Evans, I found the chair that God designed for me. And so I stayed there for almost thirty years.

All the while that I thought I was preparing to be a senior pastor, it turns out God was preparing me to be an intentional assistant. In fact, when I look back over my life, I am amazed at how God brought me to this place. Just one wrong turn, and I could have been out of it. One wrong turn and I could have missed the incomparable joy that I found being second chair to Tony Evans. But God didn't let that happen. He kept me going on the right path.

When I look at the era I came from, I can see how God placed special people in the right places to help grow me up for this ministry. I was born in New Jersey in 1941. Schools were segregated, and my little school had the first grade on one side of the room and the second grade on the other. My teachers were told that their kids couldn't read, so another student and I started showing them by reading, and we read well. That's the only reason we had books that year. Now, as a kid, I didn't understand prejudice and all those things that were happening. It was just the way things were.

But no matter the circumstances, Mrs. Perry, my kindergarten teacher, had a worldview that was perhaps bigger than anybody's I knew. Later when I went to Gloucester County College, she was on the board there. Mr. Butler, Mrs. Mills, Mrs. Tull, and Mrs. Lee, my early teachers, instilled in us the principles of working hard and working to understand all the academics we could.

God had put me in my family as the youngest of sixteen children. My mother was the consummate caring housewife. My father, Rev. Argenia Hawkins, worked in Wenonah, which was basically an all-white, small, rural community. It had all the old mansions and a glorious history, but my father, being African American, was conspicuous. Most of the time, my father had to walk back and forth to the place where he went to work. Though at times he rode home, he always had to walk to get there. Then he spent his day working in that borough of Wenonah. He was sixty-three when I was born, and he worked hard. It was very physical work. It was almost all he knew. Now I'm finally getting to the age when I'm beginning to feel what he must have been going through. He was something special.

Eventually, my father got hit on the head, lost his senses, and developed Alzheimer's. But during all those years of hard labor, he also had a love for the Lord. He even pastored our church, First Baptist of Jericho, for one year. He occasionally preached at other churches in the area when they had need of his services, but he never really wanted the front seat of being pastor, so he never pursued it.

He pursued raising us in the church, though one of my brothers and I were often called "the Sons of Thunder" like James and John in the Gospels because we were involved in so many things at First Baptist. Our pastor, Rev. W. D. Willis, recognized that we had the ability to get things done. So I worked with a little bit of everything at this church. I worked with the youth and the youth choir. I worked as janitor and set up chairs. My brother and I worked in the missionary society, we worked with the mission, and with the Sunday school. I worked with just about every aspect of that church. Eventually, I became an assistant at the church because it was the only place left for me to go.

It was really a nonpaid assistant-to-the-pastor role more than an assistant pastor position, but I cut my teeth in that volunteer spot. I drove for Reverend Willis, carried his bags, and did anything to be accessible to him and learn at his feet. And I learned his wisdom: If you stay and do it the Lord's way, the Lord will reward you. I've found that wisdom true to this day.

When I graduated from high school, I didn't think I could go to college. There was the issue of money, but there was also a counselor who told me in a face-to-face session that I'd never be college material. That troubled me deeply. With sixteen children, we weren't rich, but we were academically strong as a family. My parents made sure we always toed the mark. The girls, of course, weren't given as much of an option to go to college. They were supposed to marry and take care of their families. But my parents had wanted the boys to go. So inside, I was torn up over it, but my brother Jim just said, "Martin, you will go if you want to go."

Eventually, another brother, Gene, took a position at Gloucester County College so I was able to go and be among the first class to graduate. Having been voted "Most Likely to Expel"—rather than excel—now I have a doctorate degree.

My oldest brother also had a calming effect on my life by the manner in which he lived. I thank God for his care and concern for me. Through my many sisters and brothers who cared for me, God helped me in my development.

Even during a time that I call my "dark ages," from about eighteen to twenty-five when I was trying to find myself in all the wrong places, God worked to bring me to the role he had for me. A group came to First Baptist Church in Jericho, New Jersey. A man named Lloyd Blue made a call for all those who wanted to make a new commitment of their lives. So I made the new commitment and got back on the path I knew God wanted me to walk.

I knew that a friend named Ron Roberts was attending Dallas Theological Seminary, so I asked him to send me a catalog. I saw the summer courses for the M.A. in biblical studies, and I thought, *I can do that.* I went to Dallas in the summer of 1975. I did well, and I knew the Lord had called me to preach. I came back a year later for the full-time master of theology program.

While I was in Dallas, I had a friend, Crawford Loritts, who was starting a church with a man named Tony Evans. So I started to work with them, but I always thought I would be going back to Jericho, New Jersey.

When I graduated from Dallas Seminary, I prepared to go back to Jericho and be Reverend Willis's intern for awhile. Maybe I would be the assistant pastor at that church or senior pastor at another church in the area. But Reverend Willis wrote me a letter saying he didn't think coming back was best for me. This was a complete reversal of all my expectations, and I didn't know what direction God was taking me. But Reverend Willis, my father in the ministry, recognized that it might be wiser to stay at Oak Cliff Bible Fellowship and build with Tony Evans. At the time, I didn't feel like I wanted that, but I trusted his wisdom. So I stayed. And here I am. History proved Reverend Willis right.

I still didn't understand what God had for me, but as I saw Oak Cliff begin to develop, I recognized that this ministry was going to be big and much larger than the average church. I began to work and put my hand to increasing the ministry. And I promised Dr. Evans one year at a time. That first year, I told him, "I'm just here for one more year," and signed a one-year contract. The next year, I did the same, and then the next and the next. Eventually, we quit talking about it, and I just served on a continuing basis.

Over time, I served in so many capacities, I can't even remember them all. I probably even served as the associate over cats and dogs in the midst of all that work. But I patiently kept trying to learn what God had in store for me, where he was leading me. In the process I became familiar with most of the positions and programs in the church. That was part of God's plan, too. That familiarity served me well.

Then, as my role evolved into Dr. Evans's assistant pastor, as opposed to an associate over a particular ministry, that's where I began to find my passion. And I finally began to realize that perhaps I didn't want to become a senior pastor after all. God began to increase my understanding of who he made me to be. He took this fellow who had been trying to play in the violin section, who kept thinking he would become concertmaster only to find himself playing second fiddle, and he stood me before a mirror. And do you know what I saw? I didn't look like a violin. I could make music but not with a bow and strings. I wasn't even made of wood. I was a brass horn.

With that understanding, I became no longer a "want-to-be" servant; I became a "here-am-I" servant. My ego quit being tied up in my position and thrived by fulfilling my passion. I realized that as much as I like preaching, I didn't want to preach every Sunday. I didn't have the hunger that deeply. Dr. Evans, now, you wake him up at three o'clock in the morning and he'll say, "Where's the pulpit? Give me the pulpit." As for me, I got excited about designing the programs to support his preaching. I could see what he was preaching, organize it, put flesh on it, and put legs on it. When I saw that I had that ability, I began to be fueled by hearing his vision, writing it up, and turning it into a program.

I began to see that *I was necessary* for this ministry. The Lord was using me just as much as he was using Dr. Evans, only in a different way. God put me here to use my gifts to turn the enormous vision he was giving Dr. Evans into a workable ministry. I could have pastored a church on my own and have done well. God gave me the skills to do that. But that's not where he intended me to be. He intended for me to use those skills to support a man to whom he had given the wherewithal to lead me, to build a church with such a large mission that it would take two men to do the job normally assigned to just one. He gave Tony Evans one part; he gave me a different part. Along with the rest of our orchestra, we play together to create a beautiful harmony.

Best of Both Worlds

And I've got to tell you, I thought this part in the orchestra was the best place in the world. I had many opportunities to preach, but I didn't *have* to preach. I had authority, but the buck didn't always stop with me. I had freedom and responsibility to mentor others, yet I also had Dr. Evans right there mentoring me. I didn't have to go outside our church to find that—or to keep from being lonely at the top like senior pastors must. Dr. Evans's vision took me farther than I ever thought I would go, yet I found room for my vision within his.

God designed me for that place, that position, that orchestra. Where God takes you—the place that he designs you for—that's the best place, whether it's at a megachurch or a rural country church, or any other assignment; it's his place for you.

My expectations were to lead by pastoring in the head role, but my calling was to follow. So I had to follow my calling. And as I did, I found, to quote Jesse Jackson, "I am somebody." I was not second best; I was *the* best God had to offer for that second position. Following God's lead is all that matters.

Chapter Twelve

Symphony in Motion

And I looked, and I heard the voice of many angels around
the throne and the living creatures and the elders; and the
number of them was myriads of myriads, and thousands of
thousands, saying with a loud voice, "Worthy is the Lamb
that was slain to receive power and riches and wisdom
and might and honor and glory and blessing." And every
created thing which is in heaven and on the earth and
under the earth and on the sea, and all things in them,
I heard saying, "To Him who sits on the throne, and to
the Lamb, be blessing and honor and glory and dominion
forever and ever." And the four living creatures kept saying,
"Amen." And the elders fell down and worshiped.
(Rev. 5:11)

Second chair is not second best. Second chair is a supportive role that allows senior pastors the freedom to be

the best preachers and teachers they can be. Second chair is a connection with the congregation that makes certain the biblical principles taught in the church can be caught and learned. Second, third, and fourth chairs are God-ordained leadership roles that will help transform the body of Christ into a heavenly kingdom.

The body of Christ needs associate and assistant pastors. We need people who understand their calling and their design, who can complement a staff and a senior pastor, who can help grow believers for the kingdom. We as the body also need to learn to appreciate associates and assistants, to help them find a stable and vibrant place in the church. As long as we treat associates—and even volunteers—as second best, we are not following our Lord's example.

The role of the assistant is growing in our country. We need to prepare people in our seminaries and our Bible institutions for the challenge. We need to prepare senior pastors and assistants to function in multistaff ministries. We need to educate our congregations to appreciate and compensate assistants and associates for the important work they do alongside the senior pastor. We need to learn to walk with humility and in unity, allowing each person to say, in Christ, "I am somebody."

But ultimately, it's not about the associate himself. It's not about the senior pastor and his needs. It's not even about the local church. When the great Conductor lifts his baton to begin the final movement, when the lights in the orchestra hall darken, and the stage lights beam on the musicians, we'll find that the spotlights aren't shining from the catwalk above the stage but from the heights of heaven. The first note won't be the mellow tremble of the violin or the clear stridence of the trumpet. As the Conductor calls for the music to begin, the heavens will open—and the first note will be the awed intake of breath at the majesty of everything before us.

Then the music played on our little stage will mingle with the exquisite symphony of myriads of angels and the testimony of the elders and saints. The congregation will no longer be those who fit in the orchestra hall but children of God, as far as one can see on earth and in heaven, lifting their voices in unison.

If you follow your calling well, perhaps, like Stephen in the early days of the church, you'll catch a glimpse of our Savior standing to welcome you, and to give ovation for a job well done. But whether you are wearing tuxedo tails or rags, no one else will be looking at you. Mesmerized by the music, beautiful beyond any you've ever heard before, suddenly you will realize that being second chair was *never* about you, or who you are or your worth. It was never about being noticed or recognized. It was never about reaching a certain level of success or about having your say or your way. Second chair was never even about a job.

Second chair is not second best. Second chair is not second fiddle to a senior pastor. Second chair is really not even a brass horn. Second chair is the Son of God seated on the throne of honor, with a crown of glory, to whom we sing, "Worthy is the Lamb that was slain to receive power and riches and wisdom and might and honor and glory and blessing" (Rev. 5:12). It's not about us. And it's not second best. May God be with you as you perform his will—in the first chair . . . or the second.

Afterword

*A*s you continue on your way to discovering or confirming your design and your calling, you may wish to have access to other materials and supportive relationships that will help you refine your understanding of the assistant pastor role. We would like to help.

If you are interested in information about an association for assistant and associate pastors, or if you want to receive other resources for associates and assistants about leadership and other topics, please send a 3" x 5" index card with your name, phone number, and address indicating your interest to:

Metro Discipling Ministries

P.O. Box 765287, Dallas, TX 75376

You may also call: 972-723-1569 or 972-723-2910.

Notes

Introduction

1. Chris Smith, "Sweet Music from a Second Fiddle," *Leadership* 2, no. 4 (1990): 66.

2. Although I believe there are places for women in ministry, especially concerning the mentoring of other women, because of personal doctrinal beliefs pertaining to women and the senior pastorate, I am largely addressing this book to men in the ministry.

3. Smith, "Sweet Music," 66.

Chapter One: Second Chair

1. Lyle E. Schaller, *Twenty-One Bridges to the 21ˢᵗ Century* (Nashville: Abington Press, 1995), 24.

2. Donald R. Esa, "Issues in Ministry Effectiveness for the Associate Pastor" (Th.D. dissertation, Fuller Theological Seminary, 1996), 1.

3. Anthony T. Evans, interview with author, Dallas, Texas, November 9, 1999.

4. Brad Smith, interview with Donald R. Esa, "Issues in Ministry Effectiveness for the Associate Pastor" (Th.D. dissertation, Fuller Theological Seminary, 1996), 127–28.

Chapter Three: Designed for the Second Chair ... or for Concertmaster?

1. Characteristics taken from discussion in Philip P. Scmunk, "Running the Race in Second Place: How to Be a Winning Associate Pastor" (D.Min. dissertation, Western Conservative Baptist Seminary, 1995), 70–79.

2. Ibid., 80–82.

3. For a good resource on this subject, you can order Mels Carbonell's *Uniquely You in Christ,* 1997, a personality and gift profile from your local Christian bookstore.

4. Kevin E. Lawson, Ed.D., "Thriving in Associate Staff Ministry" (report presented at the NAPCE Conference at Talbott Seminary, October 17, 1997), 10.

Chapter Four: Knowing the Score

1. Robert J. Radcliffe, *Effective Ministry as an Associate Pastor: Making Beautiful Music as a Ministry Team* (Grand Rapids: Kregel, 1998), 70.

Chapter Five: Maintaining the Orchestra

1. Lyle E. Schaller, *Survival Tactics in the Parish* (Nashville: Abington Press, 1977), 166–75.

2. Esa, "Issues in Ministry Effectiveness," 30–31.

3. Donald J. Sevetson, "The Life Cycle of Staff Relationships in the Two-Minister Church," *Christian Ministry* (November 1970): 10.

4. Ibid.

5. Dennis Fields, "Giants Growing Giants," *Fundamentalist Journal* 4, no. 7 (1985): 17.

6. Sevetson, "Life Cycle," 10.

7. Schaller, *Survival Tactics,* 175.

8. Esa, "Issues in Ministry Effectiveness," 36–37.

9. Sevetson, "Life Cycle," 12.

10. Fields, "Giants Growing Giants," 17.

11. Sevetson, "Life Cycle," 10.

12. James Berkley, "How Pastors and Associates Get Along," *Leadership* 7, no. 1 (1986): 110.

13. Fields, "Giants Growing Giants," 18.

14. Howard G. Hendricks and William Hendricks, *As Iron Sharpens Iron: Building Character in a Mentoring Relationship* (Chicago: Moody Press, 1995), 25–30.

15. Anonymous response from a Dallas Theological Seminary alum to questionnaire by Martin E. Hawkins, "Evaluation of the Assistant/ Associate Position, Doctor of Ministry Applied Research Project," 2001.

Chapter Seven: Discord

1. Jesse Sanchez, "A-Rod-for-Soriano Trade Completed." www.texas.rangers.mlb.com. Article written/posted February 16, 2004, 10:15 PM ET; article accessed April 29, 2004.

Chapter Nine: Worn Strings

1. L. Andrew Pryor, "When Your Work Goes Unnoticed," *Leadership* 2, no. 3 (1990): 36–37.

2. Smith, "Sweet Music," 68.

3. Ibid.

4. Charles T. Hindman, "The Associate Pastor's Role," *The Christian Ministry* 15, no. 3 (May 1984): 18.